New Directions for
Adult and Continuing
Education

Susan Imel
Jovita M. Ross-Gordon
COEDITORS-IN-CHIEF

D1552881

Possible Selves and Adult Learning: Perspectives and Potential

Marsha Rossiter

EDITOR

Number 114 • Summer 2007

Jossey-Bass
San Francisco

POSSIBLE SELVES AND ADULT LEARNING: PERSPECTIVES AND POTENTIAL
Marsha Rossiter (ed.)
New Directions for Adult and Continuing Education, no. 114
Susan Imel, Jovita M. Ross-Gordon, Coeditors-in-Chief

Microfilm copies of issues and articles are available in 16mm and 35mm, as well as microfiche in 105mm, through University Microfilms Inc., 300 North Zeeb Road, Ann Arbor, Michigan 48106-1346.

NEW DIRECTIONS FOR ADULT AND CONTINUING EDUCATION (ISSN 1052-2891, electronic ISSN 1536-0717) is part of The Jossey-Bass Higher and Adult Education Series and is published quarterly by Wiley Subscription Services, Inc., A Wiley Company, at Jossey-Bass, 989 Market Street, San Francisco, California 94103-1741. Periodicals Postage Paid at San Francisco, California, and at additional mailing offices. POSTMASTER: Send address changes to New Directions for Adult and Continuing Education, Jossey-Bass, 989 Market Street, San Francisco, California 94103-1741.

SUBSCRIPTIONS cost $80.00 for individuals and $195.00 for institutions, agencies, and libraries.

EDITORIAL CORRESPONDENCE should be sent to the Coeditors-in-Chief, Susan Imel, ERIC/ACVE, 1900 Kenny Road, Columbus, Ohio 43210-1090, e-mail: imel.l@osu.edu; or Jovita M. Ross-Gordon, Southwest Texas State University, EAPS Dept., 601 University Drive, San Marcos, TX 78666.

Cover photograph by Jack Hollingsworth@Photodisc

Wiley Bicentennial Logo: Richard J. Pacifico

www.josseybass.com

CONTENTS

EDITOR'S NOTES

The purpose of this volume of New Directions for Adult and Continuing Education is to introduce practitioners, scholars, and students to the construct of possible selves and its potential applications in the field of adult education. The idea of possible selves was introduced by psychologists Hazel Markus and Paula Nurius in the 1980s as a way of conceptualizing future-oriented self-images. In brief, possible selves are an individual's conceptions of future selves, including the selves that are ideal and hoped for, as well as those possible selves that one fears or dreads. The concept of possible selves encompasses both the culturally determined and the self-constructed aspects of the self. During the past twenty years, a substantial body of research has explored the connections between possible selves and life span development, race and gender, career development, and academic achievement. As a result, a variety of possible selves approaches has been applied in corresponding fields of practice. It seems clear that an understanding of possible selves—their role in transitional learning, their influence on goal directed behavior and their connection with well-being over the life course—will be fruitful for practicing adult educators. However, possible selves remain a relatively unknown construct in adult education. This volume outlines in practical terms the research-based applications of possible selves that have relevance for adult educators.

In Chapter One, I provide an overview of the possible selves construct and briefly review selected literature that applies possible selves to life span development and career transitions. In addition, I describe a qualitative exploration of the role of adult teaching and learning relationships in fostering the possible selves of adult learners. The experiences of adult learners give specificity to the process of possible selves elaboration in the context of educational helping relationships.

In Chapter Two, Angeliki Leondari sets the stage for our consideration of possible selves and adult learning by providing an overview of the connections between future-oriented self-conceptualizations and academic achievement. Her chapter offers a useful review of research literature that ties future time perspectives of the self with goal achievement, particularly in the academic domain.

In the next three chapters, the authors report on research that relates possible selves to areas of interest to adult educators. Laura King and Joshua Hicks, in Chapter Three, discuss possible selves in terms of life-changing

events that require a reframing of future goals as well as relinquishment of past goals. The life event they focus on primarily is getting a divorce after more than twenty years of marriage. Their discussion of the capacity to embrace new possible selves and let go of the past has particular relevance to the practice of adult education given the well-established connection between life events and participation in educational programs among adults. In Chapter Four, Shawna Lee and Daphna Oyserman focus on the possible selves of low-income women as related to educational goals. As they point out, increasing numbers of adult nontraditional students are returning to education programs in pursuit of career advancement and employment opportunities. These authors highlight the importance of balance between positive and negative possible selves as well as the importance of connecting future possible selves to current activities. Next, in Chapter Five, Hilary Lips makes the connection between possible selves and the low representation of women in science and technology careers. She points out that it is not academic ability or academic performance but the ability to see oneself in a future role that has an impact on steering women away from careers in these fields.

The next two chapters focus on practical applications of the possible selves construct. In Chapter Six, Geoff Plimmer and Alison Schmidt describe the application of possible selves to the process of career transition. They offer a useful five-step approach to helping persons develop and elaborate new career related possible selves. And in Chapter Seven, Sarah Fletcher describes her work with preservice teachers and the uses of visualization in the mentoring relationship. Both chapters will be useful to practicing adult educators.

Finally, in Chapter Eight, I identify three considerations from the preceding chapters pertaining to the availability of possible selves for an individual, the motivational power of possible selves, and strategies to foster positive possible selves. I also discuss the implications of possible selves for our understanding of transformative learning the processes of transition.

The authors of Chapters Two through Seven are well-known scholars or practitioners whose work over the past decade has helped to define the possible selves construct in relation to adult development, academic achievement, mentoring, career development, and gender issues. They offer a diversity of perspectives from various disciplines, ideological stances, and geographical regions of the world. I am extremely honored that these individuals have contributed to this volume. Finally, I wish to express my gratitude to the New Directions for Adult and Continuing Education series editors, Susan Imel and Jovita Ross-Gordon, for their encouragement and patience, and to Katherine Chase for her capable assistance with the preparation of this manuscript.

I hope that this volume will create an increased awareness of the possible selves construct among adult educators and stimulate further dialogue regarding its potential applications in our field.

Marsha Rossiter
Editor

MARSHA ROSSITER is assistant vice chancellor for lifelong learning and community engagement at the University of Wisconsin Oshkosh.

1

The possible selves construct is presented as a useful and largely untapped perspective on adult learning. Special attention is given to the role of educational helping relationships in fostering positive possible selves among adult learners.

Possible Selves: An Adult Education Perspective

Marsha Rossiter

Adult education is about possibility. Financial self-sufficiency, personal growth, career advancement, empowerment, self-worth, and transformation are among the goals named by students and teachers alike in this field. Those goals are expressions of possibility: hope, expectation, potential. Our field is deeply rooted in the belief that learning and development are ever present, in actuality or potentiality, throughout every person's life span. We understand, as Dewey (1938) and Lindeman (1926/1961) and others did, that education is not preparation for life; it is life. All lived experience is the classroom for continuous learning and growth. With Vaill (1996), we know that learning is a way of being in the world that describes our capacity to respond constructively to the constant change in our lives. It is the capacity to find the potential for learning in every new event and iteration of our environment. As we live, we learn our way into new possibilities for ourselves.

Possible Selves

The possible selves construct offers a useful and largely unexplored framework for understanding adult learning as the medium through which change, growth, and goal achievement occur throughout the life course. Introduced by Hazel Markus and Paula Nurius in 1986, *possible selves* refer to the future-oriented components of the self-concept. Possible selves are an individual's conceptions of future selves, including the selves that are ideal and hoped for,

NEW DIRECTIONS FOR ADULT AND CONTINUING EDUCATION, no. 114, Summer 2007 © 2007 Wiley Periodicals, Inc.
Published online in Wiley InterScience (www.interscience.wiley.com) • DOI: 10.1002/ace.252

as well as those possible selves that one fears or dreads. Although possible selves reflect a future orientation, they are closely connected with both past and present self-concept. Past self-representations are an influence on possible selves to the extent that the past self will be reactivated in certain situations. For example, a past self as an unsuccessful student will lead to a similar future self-representation when that individual enters an educational setting, but it may not be an active component of the working self-concept in other situations. Of course, some past selves are not intermittent as possible selves but remain an active influence across the life span.

Possible selves also function as a context for the interpretation of the current self. That is, an individual gives a particular meaning and value to self-relevant events of the present in the light of particular hoped-for future selves. For example, the publication of a paper in a refereed journal would have a different meaning for the pretenure assistant professor for whom an important possible self is tenured professor than it would for a professor emeritus for whom an important possible self is novelist. What is significant is not necessarily the achievement of a particular possible self, but rather that the presence of the possible self constitutes a backdrop or standard against which a current self-conceptualization is evaluated.

The idea of possible selves derives from a view of the self-concept as dynamic, complex, contextually interactive, and evolving. According to this view, an individual at any time holds an array of potential self-conceptions based on her or his past experiences, broad sociocultural life context, and the current situation. Those self-conceptions vary according to valence, temporal placement, level of elaboration, and accessibility (Markus and Nurius, 1986). The working self-concept consists of that set of self-conceptions that are currently active in one's thinking and may be dominated by positive or negative possible selves at any particular time. It is important to note that an individual's repertoire of possible selves is not just any assortment of roles or identities that one can imagine, but includes only those possible selves that are psychologically accessible and personally meaningful. Current social comparisons, as well as an individual's cultural and life context, are factors in one's assessment of what might be a possible self. Within that scope, one can select which possible selves one wishes to embrace and bring to actuality, and which possible selves one wishes to resist. As such, the concept of possible selves encompasses both culturally determined and self-constructed aspects of the self.

Possible selves can be understood as an essential link between self-concept and motivation (Markus and Nurius, 1986). As representations of the self in possible future states, they give form, specificity, direction, and imagery to an individual's goals, aspirations, or fears (Markus and Nurius, 1986). For example, a positive possible self for a student who aspires to earn a degree will include vivid images of herself having achieved the goal. Perhaps she will envision herself at graduation, framing her diploma, or accepting a promotion at work. Through this imaging and elaboration, positive possible self-constructions serve to bridge the distance between the current state and a desired end state. Markus and Ruvolo (1989) suggest that possible selves are the "cognitive/affective elements that incite and direct one's self-relevant actions" and as such bring us "phenomenologically very close to the actual thoughts and feelings that individuals experience as they are in the process of motivated behavior" (p. 217). The possible selves construct views the self system as central to motivated, goal-directed behavior. The ability to construct a well-elaborated possible self around a particular goal—that is, the ability to envision oneself performing or having achieved the goal—leads to goal-directed action. Put another way, the likelihood of achieving a desired end depends in part on the ability to keep the associated successful possible self as an operative component of the working self-concept (Markus and Ruvolo, 1989; Lee and Oyserman, Chapter Four, this volume).

As an introduction to possible selves, the following section offers a brief review of research that relates possible selves to areas that are of particular interest to adult educators. Following that review is a discussion of the connection between the possible selves of adult learners and their relationships with teachers, advisers, and mentors.

Possible Selves and Life Span Development. One strand of investigation over the past two decades has looked at possible selves across the life span and their relationship to indicators of psychological well being. Markus and Nurius (1986) established the link between an individual's operative possible selves and current affective states. More recently, Cameron's research (1999) indicates that possible selves are influenced by social group membership, and psychological well-being in turn is related to the perceived group-derived efficacy—the belief that group membership will help one achieve a hoped-for self. A study of possible selves among four different age groups by Cross and Markus (1991) confirmed that possible selves are operative across the life span but provided evidence that the number of possible selves that individuals envision declines with age. Not surprisingly, there are differences in the content or focus of possible selves across age groups. Younger adults' possible selves are more likely to center on occupation and family, while older people tend to name possible selves having to do with physical and health issues. In addition, the older groups reported a lower sense of efficacy than younger groups with respect to bringing into actuality a hoped-for self or preventing a feared possible self. This is probably due to the nature of the possible selves named by different age groups (Cross and Markus, 1991). That is, the possible selves mentioned by older persons (for example, being widowed) tended to be less controllable than those named by younger persons (for example, getting a 3.5 grade point average).

Older adults, however, do not report lower life satisfaction, according to Ryff (1991). Her work offers evidence that the primary mode of self-evaluation shifts across the life span from social comparison to temporal comparison. She investigated temporal comparisons of perceived gains and losses in life of three adult age groups. The important point, with respect to life satisfaction, is that the discrepancy between ideal hoped-for possible selves and actual selves decreases with age. In Ryff's study, the oldest age group showed the least discrepancy, due primarily to lowered ideal selves. They tend to criticize themselves less harshly and accept imperfections more readily into their best hoped-for selves. Moreover, the activities to support the achievement of hoped-for possible selves are more developed and implemented by older adults than by younger (Hooker, 1999). The evidence also suggests that possible selves in later life are more individually motivated and less governed by normative or cultural expectations. Nevertheless, a recent longitudinal study of possible selves among older people reveals a high level of continuity across a five-year period. That is, both positive and negative possible selves tended to be stable rather than unstable (Frazier, Hooker, Johnson, and Kaus, 2000). As King and Hicks (Chapter Three, this volume) explain, well-being is related to the ability to let go of lost possible selves, as well as to the psychological availability of positive new possible selves.

Possible Selves and Career Development. Another area of research has applied the possible selves construct to career development and transition. Ibarra's research (1999) has explored the processes through which people adapt to and grow into new career roles. She uses the idea of provisional selves to describe temporary ways of being that people try out as they move from their current capacities and self-conceptualizations into those associated with the new role. It is a process of negotiation, not strictly adaptation, as persons attempt to find the fit between their own repertoire and the demands and expectations of the new role. Ibarra's research points to a model of adaptation as the construction of possible selves, characterized by three areas of activity: (1) observing role models to develop a repertoire of possible selves, (2) experimenting with provisional selves, and (3) evaluating the new self conceptions against internal and external standards. Possible selves serve to guide an individual's social comparisons, self-assessment, and observational and experiential learning in the transition. As Ibarra (2003) notes, "During a career transition, our possible selves spur us to find role models whom we'd like to become (and whom to avoid becoming) and help us to benchmark our progress toward those ideals. The more vivid these possible selves become, the more they motivate us to change. Why? Because we strive to become more and more like our ideals, and we scare ourselves out of becoming our most dreaded selves" (p. 38).

The possible selves construct has been fruitfully applied in the practice of career counseling (Meara, Davis, and Robinson, 1997; Meara, Day, Chalk, and Phelps, 1995). Martz (2001) suggests that counselors can increase their empathic response to the client by shifting perspectives among the hoped-for, expected, and feared possible selves. Possible selves encourage the exploration of various perspectives on the self; the client benefits through observation of the counselor's shift among different perspectives. Plimmer, Smith, Duggan, and Englert (1999–2000) point out that the possible selves approach in career counseling is effective because it "encourages a long term perspective, aids in the development of the self concept, provides information on relationships between the self and the outer world, and emphasizes the future rather than the past" (p. 87). (Plimmer and Schmidt expand on those findings in Chapter Six, this volume.)

In a related vein, the possible selves perspective has been applied to professional development (Fletcher 2000). Building on the work of Ruvolo and Markus (1992), Fletcher has explored the uses of visualization by mentors of preservice teachers as a means of stimulating the development of positive professional possible selves among the mentees. Encouraging the teachers to envision teaching situations, both past and future, and to mentally rehearse strategies for successfully responding to those situations enables them to develop toward their hoped-for professional selves. In Chapter Seven of this volume, Fletcher discusses her work with teachers using visualization in the mentoring relationship as a means to elaborate professional possible selves. Finally, the possible selves perspective has been applied also to issues of gender and race in connection with career choice (Lips, 2000; Segal, DeMeis, Wood, and Smith, 2001). In Chapter Five of this volume, Lips offers important insights related to gender influences on academic and professional possible selves.

Possible Selves and the Helping Relationship in Adult Education

Most of the possible selves research to date has not focused specifically on adult learners or adult education. However, in my work, I have conducted some preliminary exploration of the ways in which teaching and mentoring relationships in adult education influence the possible selves of returning adult college students (Rossiter, 2004). To set the stage for the discussions of possible selves in subsequent chapters, this section describes some key insights from that work. Beginning with the recognition that adult teaching and learning are relational activities (Daloz, 1986; Brookfield, 1991; Rossiter, 1999) and with the understanding that returning adult students are often in a period of transition in their careers or personal lives (Aslanian, 2001; Kasworm, Polson, and Fishback, 2002), two conclusions seem clear. First, many adult learners are in the process of exploring new possibilities for themselves, and second, teachers, mentors, and advisers are in a pivotal role to facilitate their exploration. With those assumptions, the purpose of my study was to gain deeper understanding of the impact of educational helping relationships on adult students' repertoire of possible selves. This qualitative study was limited in scope and therefore must be considered in that light, but it suggests three primary interfaces between an adult learner's interactions with educational helpers (teachers, mentors, and advisers) and their positive possible selves. In the following sections, I briefly discuss each of the three and share the voices of adult learners, whose words bring into focus the power and process of the development of possible selves.

New Possibilities. First, educational helping relationships can be the source of new positive possible selves for adult students. Some participants reported that interactions with teachers and mentors were, in their experience, the point of origin for a possible self as they became aware of new options for themselves. Sometimes a comment or suggestion from a teacher planted the seed for an entirely new possibility that the student had not previously considered. One student, for example, explained how one of her teachers introduced her to the possibility of becoming an audiologist:

> When I initially went back to school, I thought well maybe I'll try, like, to be a teacher—a biology teacher. I love the sciences; I thought, great, I love kids. So I thought well that will work. So I took a lot of science classes and . . . my biology professor at that time said, "Look, you're, you've got maybe three wrong out of all these exams you've taken. You're doing great. What are you doing? What are you going to do with your life?" And I, I was like well I thought I'd go back to school and be a biology teacher. He's like, "You know I'm a teacher." And he goes, "And it's great, but I think there's more for you." . . . He didn't think I would, I would meet my potential. . . .
>
> So he wanted me to, to check out a few um, science-related fields. And he mentioned physical therapy, and he mentioned, um—he had just had a hearing test done across the way, here on campus—and said check out this department, the audiology and speech. He mentioned a few at that time, but I don't remember them. They weren't an interest to me, so I don't remember.
>
> But physical therapy I respect, but I don't, I know I couldn't do the physics. I didn't do well in physics in high school. . . . It was like I didn't get it, so I thought I'm never going to pass it in college if I didn't get it in high school. So as much as I thought that would be a really neat field to get into I, I didn't think I could, I think it was above me. Oh, so I thought, oh okay, and so I went across the way [to the audiology program office] and met the professor there.

This student had never before considered this possibility, but the teacher's enthusiasm, knowledge, and encouragement motivated her to investigate this as a potential career. His suggestion was, of course, not sufficient to create this possible self for the learner, but it was a necessary component to opening the way to a new option for her. She discards the physical therapist possible self as not feasible. She feels it is "above her." But the audiologist possible self does seem possible to her. When I talked with her, she was near completion of her baccalaureate degree and on her way to a graduate program in audiology.

In other students' experiences, an educator's support can reawaken and reactivate a goal that the learner earlier embraced but considered unattainable.

New Directions for Adult and Continuing Education • DOI: 10.1002/ace

This is often the case with students who have experienced setbacks in the achievement of their goals or who have had little positive feedback from key support people in the past. They have given up on a previous goal, leaving it on the scrap pile of abandoned dreams. But the combination of incremental success, perseverance, and focused encouragement from a teacher or mentor can enable a student to resurrect a lost possible self.

In still another variation of how educational relationships can be the source of possible selves, a suggestion by a teacher or mentor may be dismissed by the student at the time it is made, but later it surfaces in the student's mind to reinforce an emerging possible self. One student tells about how he had the goal of becoming a veterinarian. During this period in his studies, one of his teachers suggested that he would be a very good teacher. But because the student was focused on his goal to become a veterinarian, he did not attend to the teacher's suggestion. However, two years later, due to various circumstances, this student had moved away from his desire to be a veterinarian. He began to explore teaching, and as he did so, the earlier encouragement from his former teacher came to his consciousness as reinforcement for his newly emerging possible self.

Elaboration. A second finding was that educational relationships function as the context within which adult learners' existing positive possible selves can be elaborated, detailed, and more fully developed. Interactions with teachers and mentors offer students information that enables them to fill in the details of a tentative possible self. With specifics that pertain to a possible self, students can embellish the picture of themselves having achieved it. It seems obvious that teachers and mentors provide information about potential career possibilities to students, but the frequency with which students in my study mentioned the value of such information sharing calls attention to the pivotal role of such interaction in the students' development of a possible self.

In addition to information shared by teachers and mentors, observational learning is an important means through which students develop a possible self. Through observation of key educational helpers and role models, students assessed the goodness of fit between what they observed and what they aspired to for themselves. In the excerpt below, Dan considers his future as a high school science teacher. He describes one of his college teachers in relation to his own vision of himself as a teacher:

> [He is] an excellent physicist, very knowledgeable. . . . He's getting close to retirement and but, he's still got that, that fire for teaching. He's really a very good teacher I think. He's still motivated, he's still interested and he's always excited about class—even though we don't study as much as we should in the class and we do, do horrible on an exam or if we don't get a concept, he's, you know, he's, it doesn't, it hasn't discouraged him over the years. And I see that in him, and that, that, interest in teaching and the drive to continue and be

an excellent teacher—that just shows me that there's something to the field, to the career—of teaching that's fulfilling and motivating and stimulating at the same time. . . . It's that stimulation, that, that fulfillment that I was looking for too.

We see in Dan's story his description of qualities that he admires in his teacher, and he relates them to his own aspirations.

This dynamic works in both positive and negative directions. That is, when students admired a particular teacher, they use that teacher's behaviors and attitudes as a guide to their fuller development of a positive possible self. And they also use the behaviors of teachers they do not admire as negative possible selves they wish to avoid. Helen's story illustrates the process of sifting through potential goals, rejecting her first goal and finding another. Her original goal was to become a science teacher, until she observed her own science professor:

It seemed like with science I'm pretty textbook smart, where if I read something I can remember it and recall it. And so I had fun with some of the classes here and I just thought that was the direction that I wanted to move in, I guess. But as I got into what I would really be doing as a teacher of science, it just kind of became apparent that it wouldn't be something that I would enjoy. Um, I guess, um, starting to take the classes that had the laboratory stuff and, you know, just starting to think about—Can I see myself in that, in that professor's position? . . . I guess I started to realize then that I just didn't fit that. I didn't fit that measurement and now hold this up and now I've got to clean up the lab [laughs]. I'm not much of a cook either so probably you know the whole thing just . . . [did not appeal].

The educational relationship provides the context in which students could try out different professional identities. The opportunity to practice the values and culture of a particular career is an important step toward refining the possible self.

Efficacy Beliefs. A third finding from this exploration is that educational relationships serve to strengthen confidence and efficacy beliefs in relation to positive possible selves for adult learners. Here an understanding of possible selves is important because the experience described by students in this study does not simply entail a teacher trying to bolster the student's self-esteem. It is instead a process through which the teacher details a possible self, enabling the student to form a more fully elaborated picture of that possibility. Also critical is the role of the teacher or mentor in assisting the student to identify proximal goals and specific strategies to achieve those short-term steps. The teacher or mentor helps the student to anticipate barriers and setbacks and plan for how to meet those difficulties when they arise. Some level of confidence on the student's part in her or his own ability to achieve a particular

New Directions for Adult and Continuing Education • DOI: 10.1002/ace

positive possible self is required to bring it to fruition. The positive and practical feedback from a trusted teacher or mentor is a potent force in strengthening that sense of efficacy for an adult learner. In the excerpt below, Denise describes the emergence of a possible self earning a doctorate. Denise is completing her second bachelor's degree and has decided to go on for a master's degree. Now, with the encouragement of a professor, she begins to envision a Ph.D. possible self:

> I talked to a professor after the semester was over and she was just really encouraging me, encouraging me to keep going and to get my Ph.D. 'Cause she really liked what I had written for her class, and the work that I had done. . . .
>
> It was, and it really felt good . . . you know, you think you can do something, but when someone else says they think you can too, it's just kind of validated. Like, "Oh, yeah, maybe I can do it." I had thought about getting a master's degree . . . and the master's degree seemed kind of abstract. You know it sounded like something I'd want to do, but I really didn't know how—now I know what and I know how. . . .
>
> The Ph.D. is a harder vision, but I think I can do it. Um, it's because I think the thought is a lot newer. You know when I think of Ph.D. I think, oh Dr. so-and-so, and then you know I try and picture the "Dr." in front of my name, and it's kind of weird. . . . You know, I've heard of all the work just involved with it and it's very, it's very frightening in that way. But I think I can do it.

A clear and consistent message from a teacher who believes in the student's ability to perform well is noted and remembered as a cornerstone of confidence, even by very competent students as they consider what is possible in the future.

An Adult Education Perspective

An adult education perspective on possible selves focuses on the areas of activity where the possible selves construct intersects with concerns of adult educators—life span development, career transition, persistence toward academic goals, and the teaching or mentoring relationship. A sizable and growing body of research demonstrates the usefulness of understanding these domains of human behavior in terms of possible selves. Our insights into adult learners' motivation, future time orientation, educational goals, and self-efficacy beliefs will be enriched by an acquaintance with the dynamics of possible selves. In the chapters that follow, the authors offer a deeper look at possible selves in a variety of settings, each with important implications for practice in adult education.

References

Aslanian, C. B. *Adult Students Today*. New York: College Board, 2001.

Brookfield, S. "Grounding Teaching in Learning." In M. W. Galbraith (ed.), *Facilitating Adult Learning: A Transactional Process*. Malabar, Fla.: Krieger, 1991.

Cameron, J. E. "Social Identity and the Pursuit of Possible Selves: Implications for the Psychological Well-Being of University Students." *Group Dynamics: Theory, Research, and Practice*, 1999, 3, 179–189.

Cross, S., and Markus, H. "Possible Selves Across the Life Span." *Human Development*, 1991, 34, 230–255.

Daloz, L. *Effective Teaching and Mentoring*. San Francisco: Jossey-Bass, 1986.

Dewey, J. *Experience and Education*. New York: Collier Books, 1938.

Fletcher, S. "A Role for Imagery in Mentoring." *Career Development International*, 2000, 5, 235–243.

Frazier, L. D., Hooker, K., Johnson, P. M., and Kaus, C. R. "Continuity and Change in Possible Selves in Later Life: A Five-Year Longitudinal Study." *Basic and Applied Psychology*, 2000, 22, 237–243.

Hooker, K. "Possible Selves in Adulthood." In T. Hess and F. Blanchard-Fields (eds.), *Social Cognition and Aging*. Orlando, Fla.: Academic Press, 1999.

Ibarra, H. "Provisional Selves: Experimenting with Image and Identity in Professional Adaptation." *Administrative Science Quarterly*, 1999, 44, 764–792.

Ibarra, H. *Working Identity: Unconventional Strategies for Reinventing Your Career*. Boston: Harvard Business School Press, 2003.

Kasworm, C. E., Polson, C. J., and Fishback, S. J. *Responding to Adult Learners in Higher Education*. Malabar, Fla.: Krieger, 2002.

Lindeman, E. C. *The Meaning of Adult Education*. New York: Harvest House, 1961. (Originally published 1926)

Lips, H. M. "College Students' Visions of Power and Possibility as Moderated by Gender." *Psychology of Women Quarterly*, 2000, 24, 39–43.

Markus, H., and Nurius, P. "Possible Selves." *American Psychologist*, 1986, 41, 954–959.

Markus, H., and Ruvolo, A. "Possible Selves: Personalized Representations of Goals." In L. A. Pervin (ed.), *Goal Concepts in Personality and Social Psychology*. Mahwah, N.J.: Erlbaum, 1989.

Martz, E. "Expressing Counselor Empathy Through the Use of Possible Selves." *Journal of Employment Counseling*, 2001, 38, 128–133.

Meara, N. M., Davis, K. L., and Robinson, B. S. "The Working Lives of Women from Lower Socioeconomic Backgrounds: Assessing Prospects, Enabling Success." *Journal of Career Assessment*, 1997, 3, 115–135.

Meara, N. M., Day, J. D., Chalk, L., and Phelps, R. E. "Possible Selves: Applications for Career Counseling." *Journal of Career Assessment*, 1995, 3, 259–277.

Plimmer, G., Smith, M., Duggan, M., and Englert, P. "Career Adaptability, Well-Being, and Possible Selves." *Career Planning and Adult Development Journal*, 1999–2000, 15, 83–92.

Rossiter, M. "Caring and the Graduate Student." *Journal of Adult Development*, 1999, 6, 205–216.

Rossiter, M. "Educational Relationships and Possible Selves in the Adult Undergraduate Experience." In R. M. Cervero, B. C. Courtenay, M. T. Hixson, and J. S. Valente (eds.), *The Cyril O. Houle Scholars in Adult and Continuing Education Program Global Research Perspectives: Volume 4*. Athens: University of Georgia, 2004.

Ruvolo, A. P., and Markus, H. R. "Possible Selves and Performance: The Power of Self-Relevant Imagery." *Social Cognition*, 1992, 10, 95–124.

Ryff, C. D. "Possible Selves in Adulthood and Old Age: A Tale of Shifting Horizons." *Psychology and Aging*, 1991, 6, 286–295.

Segal, H. G., DeMeis, D. K., Wood, G. A., and Smith, H. L. "Assessing Future Possible Selves by Gender and Socioeconomic Status Using the Anticipated Life History Measure." *Journal of Personality*, 2001, 69(1), 57–87.

Vaill, P. *Learning as a Way of Being: Strategies for Survival in a World of Permanent Whitewater*. San Francisco: Jossey-Bass, 1996.

MARSHA ROSSITER is assistant vice chancellor for lifelong learning and community engagement at the University of Wisconsin Oshkosh.

2

Possible selves and education are oriented toward future goals. This chapter surveys the literature that links possible selves achievement with motivation toward academic achievement.

Future Time Perspective, Possible Selves, and Academic Achievement

Angeliki Leondari

Goals, and by extension possible selves as personalized representations of goals, are future oriented by definition. Academic performance for most adult learners represents instrumental behavior as a strategy to achieve future life and career goals. The possible selves construct is one way of conceptualizing the temporal dimension of self-concept, based on past experiences and projecting visions of the self into the future. This chapter provides an overview of literature that outlines the concept of future time perspective as it relates to possible selves and academic performance.

Future Time Perspective and Possible Selves

Time perspective—the individual's ability to move into the past through the use of memory or to imagine the future—is considered by some theorists to be a unique human capability (Roberts, 2002). Different theories conceptualize this ability in a number of ways, including possible selves (Markus and Nurius, 1986), time perspective (Fung, Carstensen, and Lutz, 1999; Zimbardo and Boyd, 1999), temporally extended self (Moore and Lemmon, 2001), time orientation (Gjesme and Nygard, 1996), and temporal orientation (Holman and Silver, 1998). Future time perspective (FTP) is understood as the mental representation of the future, constructed by individuals at certain points in their lives, and reflecting personal and social contextual influences (Husman and Lens, 1999; Lens, 2001; Nurmi, 1991). As such, it provides a basis for setting personal goals and life plans, exploring future options, and carrying out

major decisions, all of which may affect the individual's life course (Seginer, 1992). Future time orientation, defined as a general tendency to focus on and to value the future, is a concept that has been distinguished from FTP by some researchers (for example, Lens, 1986, 2001; Nurmi, 1994), while others use the two terms interchangeably.

Future time perspective in general bears a similarity to the concept of possible selves (Markus and Nurius, 1986). Although FTP is not conceptualized as being a self-schema type construct like possible selves, it might be thought of as the construct that influences how far into the future a possible self can be projected. The terms *future time perspective, future orientation, and future possible selves* and their corresponding conceptual systems are typically subsumed within a broader focus on individuals' expectations for, or hopes and fears about, the future (Greene and Wheatley, 1992). Therefore, the terms are used interchangeably in this chapter.

Orientation to the future occurs within a certain social, cultural, and historical context that may influence conceptions of what is possible and desirable in the future (Nurmi, 1993). These conceptions function to lend meaning and organization to experiences and to motivate action by providing incentives, plans, and scripts for behavior (Cantor and Zirkel, 1990; Markus and Wurf, 1987; Oyserman, Gant, and Ager, 1995). The person who has a well-developed self-representation in a particular domain is better able to predict his or her future behavior in that domain (Markus, Crane, Bernstein, and Siladi, 1982); consequently, self-representations may also serve as the foundation for the development of cognitive representations of oneself in the future. Markus and Nurius (1986) have called these future-oriented self-conceptions *possible selves*. As outlined in Chapter One in this volume, possible selves represent those selves the person could become, would like to become, or is afraid of becoming (Cross and Markus, 1991; Markus and Nurius, 1986; Markus and Ruvolo, 1989). They encompass both hoped-for and feared images of the self. Hoped-for and feared selves influence affect and behavioral motivation in different ways. Hoped-for selves have been positively associated with performance (Higgins, 1997; Markus and Ruvolo, 1989) and behavioral motivation (Hooker and Kaus, 1992). Feared selves have been associated with negative outcomes such as depression (Carver, Lawrence, and Scheier, 1999), lower life satisfaction (Ogilvie and Clark, 1992), and anxiety and guilt (Carver, Lawrence, and Scheier, 1999, 1999). To the extent that individuals value and desire the positive or hoped-for possible selves, they adjust their behavior to increase their chances of realizing those selves. To the extent that individuals are repelled by the negative or feared possible selves, they devise behavioral patterns that decrease their chances of realizing those feared selves. In other words, the choices that people make in the present are based on their desire to develop toward the person they hope to become and away from the person they fear becoming.

These imagined selves can play an important motivational role in a number of domains, including academic striving (Oyserman, Gant, and

Ager, 1995). As affect-laden self-schemas, possible selves can also contribute to overall well-being, both by virtue of their positive or negative emotional valence and as a function of the extent to which individuals perceive that they can achieve or avoid them (Markus and Nurius, 1986).

Future Time Perspective and Motivation

Future time perspective can be a powerful motivator of current behavior (Greene and DeBacker, 2004). A sense of purpose for the future is an important factor in moving individuals to engage in activities perceived to be instrumental in achieving valued future outcomes (Simmons, Dewitte, and Lens, 2000). Two aspects of FTP have been found to be of particular relevance to academic achievement: perceived instrumentality, or utility and valence (De Volder and Lens, 1982; Husman and Lens, 1999). FTP instrumentality is conceptualized as the cognitive aspect of future time perspective consisting of the ability to anticipate in the present the long-term consequences of a potential action. In other words, perceived instrumentality is an individual's recognition that his or her current behavior is instrumental to achieving a valued future goal.

Within achievement motivation theory, instrumentality has been considered similar to utility value. Eccles (1984) described utility value as "the importance of a task for some future goal that might itself be somewhat unrelated to the process nature of the task at hand" (p. 90), and contrasted it with interest value, which she described as "the inherent, immediate enjoyment one gets from engaging in an activity" (p. 89). Eccles characterizes utility value as a form of extrinsic motivation and interest value as a form of intrinsic motivation. Many studies support the importance of perceived utility of current tasks for valued future goals. Perceived instrumentality has been shown to influence educational attainment (Lens, 1987), task engagement and persistence (Lens, Simmons, and Dewitte, 2001), and task choice (Eccles, Adler, and Meece, 1984). For academic learning, recognizing instrumental situations is important for encouraging persistence in the face of challenge or boredom (Miller and Brickman, 2004). Overall, research on FTP supports the view that students with a positive perception of the instrumentality of schoolwork to reach future career goals are more motivated for school tasks, make more use of effective learning strategies, work harder, and perform better at school (Phalet, Andriessen, and Lens, 2004). While this research has focused on youth, it is clearly applicable to adult learners. Indeed, adults' preference for instrumentality, understood as the applicability and usefulness of learning, is a core assumption of andragogy (Knowles, 1984).

Valence is seen as the dynamic aspect of FTP consisting of a disposition to attribute high value to future goals. Valuing of the future, or valence, has been shown to be associated with adaptive behavior and positive motivation. The motivational importance of an individual's perception of the future is implicitly present in the concept of possible selves as he or she mediates long-term motivation and supplies direction for the achievement of a desired goal (Markus and Nurius, 1986; Markus and Ruvolo, 1989; Oyserman and Markus, 1990a; Wurf and Markus, 1991). Those selves that seem plausible and probable for one give meaning to current behavior—positive or negative—and influence the direction of current activities by enabling the person to focus attention on specific, task-relevant thoughts and to organize action (Carson, Madison, and Santrock, 1987; Cross and Markus, 1994; Markus, Cross, and Wurf, 1990). The more a possible self is valued or the more important it is to an individual, the more likely it will be related to the individual's behavior.

Several studies (Markus and Nurius, 1986; Markus and Ruvolo, 1989; Oyserman and Markus, 1990a; Oyserman and Saltz, 1993; Ruvolo and Markus, 1992) show that possible selves and aspects of possible selves are related to a variety of outcomes, such as memory, self-esteem, delinquency, and superior performance. In effect, possible selves build a bridge between the current state and the desired future self. The more vivid and elaborate the possible selves are, the more they help the individual to concentrate on task-relevant thoughts and feelings and foster a positive emotional state that is energizing. Research also supports the view that individuals with well-elaborated positive possible selves are better able to face failures. They also have access to more strategies to avoid future failures (Cross and Markus, 1994).

Self-Conceptions of Ability, Possible Selves, and Academic Achievement

The relationship between self-conceptions of ability and academic achievement has been examined in numerous studies and is well documented (Bandura, 1986; Nicholls, 1990). Students with a high *self-concept* of ability in a specific domain have higher expectations of future success (Eccles and others, 1983; Harter, 1983), persist longer on relevant tasks (Felson, 1984; Phillips, 1984), and show higher overall levels of performance than students with a low evaluation of their ability. Recent research focused on adult general equivalency diploma (GED) students in a university setting corroborates these findings. Golden (n.d.) reports that robust self-efficacy among the students and a strong sense of self were essential to the academic success of adult learners.

Markus and her colleagues (Cross and Markus, 1994; Markus, Cross, and Wurf, 1990) use the term *self-schema* to denote the structures of self-knowledge that represent an individual's school-related abilities. They maintain that competence in a domain requires not only some ability in the domain but also a self-schema for this ability. Self-schemas are thought to produce or maintain competence in a particular domain by facilitating the encoding, evaluation, and retrieval of domain-relevant information (Cross and Markus, 1994; Markus, 1977). Therefore, the individual with a self-schema in a specific ability domain is attuned to schema-relevant situations and is ready to exercise the ability when needed (Markus, 1983; Markus, Cross, and Wurf, 1990; Markus and Wurf, 1987). Similarly, Bandura's self-efficacy theory (1977) postulates that a person's beliefs regarding competence in specific domains influence choice, performance, and persistence in endeavors that require these competencies.

Individuals without a self-schema in a particular ability domain do not recognize their ability in that domain and therefore are less likely to anticipate and simulate the necessary steps for completing a desired task, especially if the task is novel or requires extensive structuring by the individual (Cross and Markus, 1994). In addition, they may fail to persist when the task is difficult and may be vulnerable to the adverse effects of negative feedback about the self in that domain (Markus, 1977).

The role of goal investment in positive human functioning is well established. Given that goals, plans, and hopes are located in the future, how individuals construct their future is an important aspect of human motivation (Nuttin and Lens, 1985). We also know that working toward valued goals is an important aspect of psychological and physical well-being (Elliot, Sheldon, and Church, 1997; Emmons and King, 1988). Research on mental simulation and visualization indicates that imagining success at one's life goals is associated with enhanced goal progress, a tighter connection between thought and action, and a sense of purpose in life. Bringing to mind a desired possible self may also foster a positive emotional state, and the desire to maintain or enhance this state is arousing or energizing (Oyserman and Markus, 1990a, Fletcher, Chapter Seven, this volume).

Schooling and education are by definition future oriented. Possible selves, the future-oriented components of the self-schema, are viewed as the components critical for putting the self into action (Oyserman and Markus, 1990b). According to Markus and colleagues (Cross and Markus, 1994), an important base for the development of possible selves related to a given ability domain is the self-schema, which provides a base of knowledge about one's ability and makes the person sensitive and responsive to relevant stimuli. Individuals with well-developed self-schemas for an ability are more action oriented on tasks related to that ability (Kuhl, 1985) and can maintain effective concentration during the task.

Implications for Adult Education

Future time perspective aligns with and expands what we know about adult learners in terms of motivation to participate in education and in relation to the role of self-efficacy. It has been argued that an individual's total motivation to learn derives in large part from the perceived instrumentality of the learning activities for the achievement of intrinsic and extrinsic goals in the near and distant future (Husman and Lens, 1999). In short, the promise of long-term rewards is a critical aspect of motivation. In adult education, we know that it is just this motivation that brings many adult learners to the educational experience; the practical value of learning has been an enduring theme in the field for decades. Beginning with Houle's (1961) typology of adult learners, goal orientation appears as a prominent factor in most of the models developed to explain participation in adult education (Merriam and Caffarella, 1999). In the context of formal education, the great majority of adult learners cite future career goals as their primary reason for returning to school (Aslanian, 2001). Recognizing the importance of future goals as a motivating factor in learning directs our attention to understanding how adult learners construct their goals and their possible selves. Past academic experience, socioeconomic status, and psychological well-being are among the factors that may limit or distort adult learners' views of what is possible for them. Furthermore, the perception of instrumentality of learning may be weak. As Kasworm's work (2003) makes clear, many adult learners in university settings experience a disconnect between the academic knowledge they are required to study and real-world knowledge. Adult educators can assist learners by helping them clarify, expand, and elaborate on realistic goals and make the connections between strategies for academic success and their future life goals.

The relationships among current self-views, possible selves, and academic outcomes have important implications for instructional practices. The construction of current and possible self-views is a dynamic process (Brown, 1998; Markus and Nurius, 1986). Thus, students are actively constructing their futures as they construct their self-views, and, reciprocally, they are actively adjusting their self-views to fit the futures they are envisioning. The link between self-efficacy and learning has clear implications for practice in adult education. Based on her study of adult GED students in college, Golden (n.d.) concludes, "Adult educators can be instrumental in how adult students approach new content areas by facilitating and encouraging a learning environment that provides positive reinforcement and rewards the learners' behaviors to increase their level of self-efficacy" (p. 16). Similarly, we know that low self-esteem and lack of confidence are barriers to academic success for many adult learners (Darkenwald and Valentine, 1985; James, 2003). To help learners envision themselves as successful learners rather than academic failures is key. Self-esteem is related to one's sense of competence—understood as a person's confidence in ability level—and a sense of worthiness, that is, confidence in one's right to be successful. The possible selves literature suggests that self-efficacy beliefs can be strengthened through the elaboration of positive future-oriented self-images. Thus, educators can have an impact on self-efficacy by reinforcing learners' tentative possible selves as successful students.

The literature on career development suggests strongly that self-views have a large impact on vocational decisions. Occupational attainment in adulthood is predicted by job aspirations and belief in one's own abilities in adolescence (Schoon, 2001). These results highlight the importance of both students' current self-evaluations and their perceptions of what is possible for them in the future. This is why it is particularly important for adult educators to be concerned with the possible selves of adult learners. Given that their views of various career and educational opportunities may have been stunted or curtailed earlier in these learners' lives, the educator's role in facilitating an expansion or transformation of the learner's sense of possibility is critical. As Rossiter (2004) has suggested, educators can assist students not only in providing information and options, but also in supplying or introducing possible aspirations concerning the future. Levels of self-efficacy in relation to academic performance can be enhanced or diminished through experience. Adult learners' goals and possible selves evolve as they develop a sense of academic empowerment (Terry, 2006). As students experience success, they become more confident and then must revisit and revise their goals. In sum, a better understanding of the role of possible selves as determinants of achievement and motivation may lead to practices that help learners to visualize their future and relate their present academic involvement with future selves (Otto, 1991; Oyserman, Terry, and Bybee, 2002).

References

Aslanian, C. B. *Adult Students Today*. New York: College Board, 2001.
Bandura, A. "Self-Efficacy: Toward a Unifying Theory of Behavioral Change." *Psychological Review*, 1977, 84, 191–215.
Bandura, A. *Social Foundations of Thought and Action: A Social Cognitive Theory*. Upper Saddle River, N.J.: Prentice Hall, 1986.
Brown, J. D. *The Self*. New York: McGraw-Hill, 1998.
Cantor, N., and Zirkel, S. "Personality, Cognition, and Purposive Behavior." In L. A. Pervin (ed.), Handbook of *Personality Theory and Research*. New York: Guilford Press, 1990.
Carson, A. D., Madison, T., and Santrock, J. W. "Relationships Between Possible Selves and Self-Reported Problems of Divorced and Intact Family Adolescents." *Journal of Early Adolescence*, 1987, 7, 191–204.
Carver, C., Lawrence, J., and Scheier, M. "Self-Discrepancies and Affect: Incorporating the Role of Feared Selves." *Personality and Social Psychology Bulletin*, 1999, 25, 783–792.
Cross, S., and Markus, H. "Possible Selves Across the Life Span." *Human Development*, 1991, 34, 230–255.
Cross, S., and Markus, H. "Self-Schemas, Possible Selves, and Competent Performance." *Journal of Educational Psychology*, 1994, 86, 423–438.
Darkenwald, G. G., and Valentine, T. "Factor Structure of Deterrents to Public Participation in Adult Education." *Adult Education Quarterly*, 1985, 35, 177–193.
De Volder, M., and Lens, W. "Academic Achievement and Future Time Perspective as a Cognitive-Motivational Concept." *Journal of Personality and Social Psychology*, 1982, 42, 566–571.
Eccles, J. "Sex Differences in Achievement Patterns." In B. Sonderegger (ed.), *Nebraska Symposium on Motivation*. Lincoln: University of Nebraska Press, 1984.
Eccles, J., Adler, T., and Meece, J. L. "Sex Differences in Achievement: A Test of Alternate Theories." *Journal of Personality and Social Psychology*, 1984, 46, 26–43.
Eccles, J., and others. "Expectancies, Values, and Academic Behaviors." In J. T. Spence (ed.), *Achievement and Achievement Motives*. New York: Freeman, 1983.

Elliot, A. J., Sheldon, K. M., and Church, M. A. "Avoidance Personal Goals and Subjective Well-Being." *Personality and Social Psychology Bulletin,* 1997, *23,* 915–927.

Emmons, R. A., and King, L. A. "Conflict Among Daily Goals: Immediate and Long-Term Implications for Psychological and Physical Well-being." *Journal of Personality and Social Psychology,* 1988, *54,* 1040–1048.

Felson, R. B. "The Effect of Self-Appraisals of Ability on Academic Performance." *Journal of Personality and Social Psychology,* 1984, *47,* 944–952.

Fung, H. H., Cartensen, L. L., and Lutz, A. M. "Influences of Time on Social Preferences: Implications for Life-Span Development." *Psychological Aging,* 1999, *14,* 595–604.

Gjesme, T., and Nygard, R. *Advances in Motivation.* Boston: Scandinavian University Press, 1996.

Golden, S. "Self-Efficacy: How Does It Influence Academic Success?" *Adult Learning,* n.d.

Greene, A. L., and Wheatley, S. M. "'I've Got a Lot to Do and I Don't Think I'll Have the Time': Gender Differences in Late Adolescents' Narratives of the Future." *Journal of Youth and Adolescence,* 1992, *21,* 667–685.

Greene, B. A., and DeBacker, T. K. "Gender and Orientations Toward the Future: Links to Motivation." *Educational Psychology Review,* 2004, *16,* 91–120.

Harter, S. "Developmental Perspectives on the Self-System." In M. Hetherington (ed.), *Handbook of Child Psychology: Socialization, Personality, and Social Development.* Hoboken, N.J.: Wiley, 1983.

Higgins, E. "Beyond Pleasure and Pain." *American Psychologist,* 1997, *52,* 1280–1300.

Holman, E. A., and Silver, R. C. "Getting 'Stuck' in the Past: Temporal Orientation and Coping with Trauma." *Journal of Personality and Social Psychology,* 1998, *74,* 1146–1163.

Hooker, K., and Kaus, C. "Possible Selves and Health Behaviors in Later Life." *Journal of Aging and Health,* 1992, *4,* 390–411.

Houle, C. O. *The Inquiring Mind.* Madison: University of Wisconsin Press, 1961.

Husman, J., and Lens, W. "The Role of the Future in Student Motivation." *Educational Psychologist,* 1999, *34,* 113–125.

James, K. "How Low Self-Esteem Affects Adult Learners." *Adults Learning,* 2003, *14,* 24–27.

Kasworm, C. "Adult Meaning Making in the Undergraduate Classroom." *Adult Education Quarterly,* 2003, *53,* 81–98.

Knowles, M. S., and others. *Andragogy in Action: Applying Modern Principles of Adult Learning.* San Francisco: Jossey-Bass, 1984.

Kuhl, J. "Volitional Mediators of Cognition-Behavior Consistency: Self-Regulatory Processes and Action Versus State Orientation." In J. Kuhl and J. Beckmann (eds.), *Action Control: From Cognition to Behavior.* New York: Springer-Verlag, 1985.

Lens, W. "Future Time Perspective: A Cognitive-Motivational Concept." In D. R. Brown and J. Veroff (eds.), *Frontiers of Motivational Psychology.* New York: Springer-Verlag, 1986.

Lens, W. "Future Time Perspective, Motivation and School Performance." In E. De Corte, J. Lodewijks, R. Parmentier, and P. Span (eds.), *Learning and Instruction: European Research in an International Context.* Leuven, Belgium and New York: Leuven University Press and Pergamon Press, 1987.

Lens, W. "How to Combine Intrinsic Task Motivation with the Motivational Effects of the Instrumentality of Present Tasks for Future Goals." In A. Efklides, J. Kuhl, and R. Sorrentino (eds.), *Trends and Prospects in Motivation Research.* Norwell, Mass.: Kluwer, 2001.

Lens, W., Simmons, J., and Dewitte, S. "Student Motivation and Self-Regulation as a Function of Future Time Perspective and Perceived Instrumentality." In S. Volet and S. Jarvela (eds.), *Motivation in Learning Contexts: Theoretical Advances and Methodological Implications.* New York: Pergamon Press, 2001.

Markus, H. "Self-Schemata and Processing Information About the Self." *Journal of Personality and Social Psychology*, 1977, *35*, 63–78.
Markus, H. "Self-Knowledge: An Expanded View." *Journal of Personality*, 1983, *51*, 543–565.
Markus, H., Crane, M., Bernstein, S., and Siladi, M. "Self-Schemas and Gender." *Journal of Personality and Social Psychology*, 1982, *42*, 38–50.
Markus, H., Cross, S. E., and Wurf, E. "The Role of the Self-System in Competence." In R. J. Sternberg and J. Kolligian Jr. (eds.), *Competence Considered*. New Haven, Conn.: Yale University Press, 1990.
Markus, H., and Nurius, N. "Possible Selves." *American Psychologist*, 1986, *41*, 954–969.
Markus, H., and Ruvolo, A. "Possible Selves: Personalized Representations of Goals." In L. A. Pervin (ed.), *Goal Concepts in Personality and Social Psychology*. Mahwah, N.J.: Erlbaum, 1989.
Markus, H., and Wurf, E. "The Dynamic Self-Concept: A Social Psychological Perspective." *Annual Review of Psychology*, 1987, *38*, 299–337.
Merriam, S. B., and Caffarella, R. S. *Learning in Adulthood: A Comprehensive Guide*. (2nd ed.) San Francisco: Jossey-Bass, 1999.
Miller, R. B., and Brickman, S. J. "A Model of Future-Oriented Motivation and Self-Regulation." *Educational Psychology Review*, 2004, *16*, 9–33.
Moore, C., and Lemmon, K. *The Self in Time: Developmental Perspectives*. Mahwah, N.J.: Erlbaum, 2001.
Nicholls, J. G. "What Is Ability and Why Are We Mindful of It? A Developmental Perspective." In R. Sternberg and J. Kolligan (eds.), *Competence Considered*. New Haven, Conn.: Yale University Press, 1990.
Nurmi, J. "How Do Adolescents See Their Future? A Review of the Development of Future Orientation and Planning." *Developmental Review*, 1991, *11*, 1–59.
Nurmi, J. "Adolescent Development in an Age-Graded Context: The Role of Personal Beliefs, Goals, and Strategies in the Tackling of Developmental Tasks and Standards." *International Journal of Behavioral Development*, 1993, *16*, 169–189.
Nurmi, J. E. "The Development of Future Orientation in a Life-Span Context." In Z. Zaleski (ed.), *Psychology of Future Orientation*. Lublin, Poland: Towarzystwo Naukowe KUL, 1994.
Nuttin, J., and Lens, W. *Future Time Perspective and Motivation: Theory and Research Method*. Leuven, Belgium, and Mahwah, N.J.: Leuven University Press and Erlbaum, 1985.
Ogilvie, D., and Clark, M. "The Best and Worst of It: Age and Sex Differences in Self-Discrepancy Research." In R. Lipka and T. Brinthaupt (eds.), *Self Perspectives Across the Lifespan*. Albany, N.Y.: SUNY Press, 1992.
Otto, L. "Today's Youth and Tomorrow's Careers: A Social Psychological Career Development Program." *Journal of Applied Psychology*, 1991, *8*, 19–35.
Oyserman, D., Gant, L., and Ager, J. "A Socially Contextualized Model of African American Identity: Possible Selves and School Persistence." *Journal of Personality and Social Psychology*, 1995, *69*, 1216–1232.
Oyserman, D., and Markus, H. "Possible Selves and Delinquency." *Journal of Personality and Social Psychology*, 1990a, *59*, 112–125.
Oyserman, D., and Markus, H. "Possible Selves in Balance: Implications for Delinquency." *Journal of Social Issues*, 1990b, *46*(2), 141–157.
Oyserman, D., and Saltz, E. "Competence, Delinquency, and Attempts to Attain Possible Selves." *Journal of Personality and Social Psychology*, 1993, *65*, 360–374.
Oyserman, D., Terry, K., and Bybee, D. "A Possible Selves Intervention to Enhance School Involvement." *Journal of Adolescence*, 2002, *25*, 313–326.
Phalet, K., Andriessen, I., and Lens, W. "How Future Goals Enhance Motivation and Learning in Multicultural Classrooms." *Educational Psychology Review*, 2004, *16*(1), 59–89.

Phillips, D. C. "The Illusion of Incompetence Among Academically Competent Children." *Child Development*, 1984, *55*, 2000–2016.

Roberts, W. A. "Are Animals Stuck in Time?" *Psychological Bulletin*, 2002, *128*, 473–489.

Rossiter, M. "Educational Relationships and Possible Selves in the Adult Undergraduate Experience." In R. M. Cervero, B. C. Courtenay, M. T. Hixson, and J. S. Valente (eds.), *The Cyril O. Houle Scholars in Adult and Continuing Education Program Global Research Perspectives: Volume 4*. Athens: University of Georgia, 2004.

Ruvolo, A. P., and Markus, H. R. "Possible Selves and Performance: The Power of Self-Relevant Imagery." *Social Cognition*, 1992, *10*, 95–124.

Schoon, I. "Teenage Job Aspirations and Career Attainment in Adulthood: A Seventeen-Year Follow-Up Study of Teenagers Who Aspired to Become Scientists, Health Professionals, or Engineers." *International Journal of Behavioral Development*, 2001, *25*, 124–132.

Seginer, R. "Future Orientation: Age-Related Differences Among Adolescent Females." *Journal of Youth and Adolescence*, 1992, *21*, 421–437.

Simmons, J., Dewitte, S. and Lens, W. "Wanting to Have Versus Wanting to Be: The Effect of Perceived Instrumentality on Goal Orientation." *British Journal of Psychology*, 2000, *91*, 335–351.

Terry, M. "Making a Difference in Learners' Lives: Results of a Study Based on Adult Literacy Programs." *Adult Basic Education*, 2006, *16*, 3–19.

Wurf, E., and Markus, H. "Possible Selves and the Psychology of Personal Growth." In D. J. Ozer, J. M. Healy, and A. J. Stewart (eds.), *Perspectives on Personality*. London: Jessica Kingsley, 1991.

Zimbardo, P. G., and Boyd, J. N. "Putting Time in Perspective: A Valid, Reliable Individual Differences Metric." *Journal of Personality and Social Psychology*, 1999, *77*, 1271–1288.

ANGELIKI LEONDARI *is associate professor in the Department of Pre-School Education at the University of Thessaly in Volos, Greece.*

New Directions for Adult and Continuing Education • DOI: 10.1002/ace

3

How do the goals we once cherished but can no longer pursue relate to maturity?

Lost and Found Possible Selves: Goals, Development, and Well-Being

Laura A. King, Joshua A. Hicks

"What do you want to be when you grow up?" is perhaps one of the most common questions adults ask children. It reveals the common human interest in goals as well as a sense that someday we all come to a place called being "grown up." Yet if there is a lesson in adulthood, it is that growing up is a process that never stops while one still draws breath. Being grown up does not mean occupying a static "happily ever after" but rather negotiating a constantly changing landscape of what might have been and what might still be. With adulthood may come the need to ask oneself the questions, "What *did* I want to be?" and, perhaps more important, "What do I hope to become?" Consider the experiences of a sample of seventy-three women at midlife, divorced after marriages of more than twenty years (King and Raspin, 2004). Some confessed to having never signed a lease, written a check, or applied for a job prior to the divorce. Many of these women had not worked outside the home in a decade or more. For many, the experience of divorce was the fruition of their worst-case scenarios. The majority reported a loss of income after the divorce, and nearly all remained single, despite experiencing the divorce, on average, nearly a decade earlier.

Prior to the divorce, many of these women imagined themselves having made it to "grown up." They had arrived at that spot on the map of their lives

Preparation of this chapter and the research described in it were supported by NIMH grant R29–54142.

NEW DIRECTIONS FOR ADULT AND CONTINUING EDUCATION, no. 114, Summer 2007 © 2007 Wiley Periodicals, Inc.
Published online in Wiley InterScience (www.interscience.wiley.com) • DOI: 10.1002/ace.254

that indicated adulthood—that imaginary stationary end point of development. For many of these women, the experience of divorce was an unexpected and traumatic event that entailed a change in their life goals. Two tasks must be completed to negotiate such a change: confronting what one has lost—what one at one time "wanted to be when she grew up"—and generating and reinvesting in new goals toward which to strive.

In our research, we have asked adults who have experienced challenging life transitions to tell us about the life goals they once sought but no longer do and those goals that motivate their lives now. These samples have included not only women who have experienced divorce after long marriage but other community samples recruited because they had experienced important and challenging life transitions, including gay men and lesbians (King and Smith, 2004) and parents of children with Down syndrome (King and Patterson, 2000). These individuals differ in many ways, but they share a common feature: all experienced a significant change in the possible self landscapes of their lives. Our research examines how adults' views of their lost and found goals relate to maturity. In this chapter, we share some of the results of these studies with a special eye toward understanding the role of possible selves in adult development, the trade-offs that might characterize maturity, and the issues facing adults who have the opportunity to grow through important challenging life experiences.

Lost and Found Possible Selves

Possible selves are personalized representations of the important life goals (Markus and Nurius, 1986; Ruvolo and Markus, 1992). Possible selves encompass not only the goals we are seeking but all of the imaginable futures we might occupy. Possible selves serve as cognitive resources that motivate the self throughout adult development (Cross and Markus, 1991). In our research, we ask participants to generate written narrative descriptions of two possible selves: their current best possible selves and an unattainable possible self that they may have once cherished or a lost possible self. Possible selves are motivational units. To the extent that possible selves (and goals in general) provide the structures through which daily events are evaluated (King, forthcoming), possible selves represent a person's construction of current and previous sources of meaning in life.

Pursuit and progress on goals is a strong predictor of psychological and physical well-being (Sheldon and Kasser, 1999; Little, 1999). To successfully negotiate a major life change—to come out on the other side of a traumatic life event—one must recommit to goals in order to restore positive functioning. Important life changes require a change in one's goals, but disengaging from previously valued goals is a difficult process that involves recognizing that one's abilities, opportunities, and life circumstances will never lead to one's hoped-for future. Relinquishing attachment to a goal requires surrendering rewards that one had previously invested with value, accepting one's mistaken expectations about the future, and perhaps reevaluating one's very place in the world. A hallmark of successful self-regulation may be the flexible pursuit of goals—disengaging from life goals that no longer include the possibility of fulfillment (King, 1996, 1998). Yet when previously cherished goals are no longer possible, people are likely to redouble their efforts rather than disengage (Emmons, Colby, and Kaiser, 1998). These results speak to the power of goals in our lives and also point to the challenge of letting go.

To measure aspects of lost and found possible selves, we asked participants in our studies to generate narrative descriptions of their previous and current goals. The instructions for the lost possible self narrative are variations on the following: "We would like you to consider your future as you imagined it *before* [the life-changing event]. Try to remember how you imagined your future to be. What sorts of things did you hope for and dream about for your life? Think of this as your 'best possible life' or your happily ever after, if you *had not experienced* [the event]." The instructions for the best found possible self narrative are the following (King and Raspin, 2004): "We would like you to consider the life you imagine for yourself currently, and in the future. What sorts of things do you hope for and dream about? Imagine that your life has gone as well as it possibly could have. You have worked hard and achieved your goals. Think of this as your 'best possible life' or your 'happily ever after.'"

Using these narrated possible selves, we examined two aspects of possible selves: salience and elaboration. *Salience* refers to the extent to which individuals think about the possible self and the ease with which it can be called to mind. A salient possible self is one that is frequently activated in the working self-concept and is chronically available to the person—a relatively constant source of motivation. Salience is measured through self-report by simply asking individuals to rate how much they currently think about that possible self, how easy it is for them to imagine, and so on.

Elaboration, in contrast, refers to the richness of the narrative the person has generated. Elaboration is reliably content-analyzed by independent raters, coding these protocols on dimensions such as elaboration, vividness, emotionality, and detail (King and Raspin, 2004; King and Smith, 2004). Excerpts from the narratives provided by women who experienced divorce after long marriages illustrate the meaning of the elaboration dimension. The following is an excerpt from a highly elaborate lost possible self:

I imagined a deliriously happy "empty nest" syndrome. Neither of us likes to travel, but sports are a big priority. I figured we would exercise, go to sporting events, theatre, etc., together. I envisioned weddings with lots of family pictures. There would be grandchildren to baby-sit. Life would be calm, easy and sweet [King and Raspin, 2004, p. 616].

New Directions for Adult and Continuing Education • DOI: 10.1002/ace

A lost possible self-narrative scoring low in elaboration follows.

> I am a realist and never expect anything from life.

Excerpts from a highly elaborate found possible self include the following:

> In my current or real life, I set goals and experience HARD work as I seek to attain them. I feel fortunate in a backhanded way to have experienced misfortune as a young woman. I feel it taught me humility, to be nonjudgmental, compassionate, and gave me the ability to regroup. Life is good but not lavish. It's hard work and we have to give each other a hand once in awhile. I have changed my goals from material to spiritual. Forgiveness has been key. I have imagined college degrees, a cozy home, educated, healthy well-adjusted children, an interesting job, a good marriage.

An excerpt from a found possible self judged to be low in elaboration follows:

> My life has been ruined by this divorce. If I no longer have a trusting partner to share dreams and goals with why even bother to have them? What good is anything without someone to share it with? My current goal is only to make enough money to make my monthly bills without withdrawing money from my savings account.

Salience and elaboration are independent aspects of narrative possible selves. An individual may be haunted by a possible self but not have a rich understanding of this future goal. For example, a divorced woman might often think about a lost possible self related to her previous marriage, without deeply considering the nuances of that forsaken life. Conversely, an individual may be able to construct a vivid description of a possible self, but not often think about that possible self much in everyday life. A woman who has experienced divorce after a long marriage might have thought deeply about her previous possible self and developed a vivid image of that lost life. After coming to the conclusion that such a life path is no longer possible (or even preferred), however, she may not often think about this once important goal.

Among divorced women, participants who initiated the divorce rated their found possible self as more salient and their lost possible self as less so. The number of years elapsed since the divorce was also negatively related to the salience of the lost possible self, suggesting that time does indeed heal some wounds (King and Raspin, 2004). After a life-changing experience, the individual faces the twofold challenge of saying good-bye to previous goals and reinvesting in a new life dream. What are the implications of each of these processes for adulthood and maturity? Before describing how the salience and elaboration of lost and found possible selves relate to adult development, a discussion of our approach to maturity is warranted.

New Directions for Adult and Continuing Education • DOI: 10.1002/ace

Well-Being and Personality Development: Two Sides of Maturity

It is difficult to imagine a person who is considered mature not also experiencing some modicum of subjective well-being. To some extent, successful aging implies happy aging, and research has shown that well-being may well increase with age (Mroczek, 2001; Mroczek and Spiro, 2005; Sheldon and Kasser, 2001). Well-being would appear to be an important aspect of maturity, but happiness is not everything. A person who is complacent in an objectively negative situation or remains blissfully ignorant of real conflict would seem to fall short of some important aspects of maturity (compassion, insight). In addition, some aspects of maturity might require the (temporary) sacrifice of happiness in favor of other developmental goals (King, 2001). Therefore, in examining the relations of possible selves to maturity, we have examined not only well-being but also personality development or, specifically, ego development.

Ego development refers to the level of complexity with which one experiences oneself and the world (Loevinger, 1976). While well-being is typically measured using quite transparent self-report ratings, ego development is measured by coding responses to the sentence completion test (Hy and Loevinger, 1996). As ego level increases, the individual's frame of reference becomes more complex. At the earliest stages of ego development, individuals are dominated by impulses, lack insight, and engage in simplistic thinking. With development, they are able to control and channel their impulses, perceiving the social world in increasingly complex ways. People at the higher stages of ego development recognize that life's lessons are contextualized and relative. They show a capacity to recognize conflict and experience ambivalence. Identity and mutuality become concerns at the highest stages. Ego development has been shown to relate to openness to experience (McCrae and Costa, 1980), increased compassion, tolerance, empathy, and the capacity for interpersonal connectedness (see Pals and John, 1998, for a review). Ego development has been described as the development of character (Westen, 1998).

Importantly, ego development is independent of well-being or psychological adjustment (Noam, 1998). Just as well-being does not capture all of the characteristics associated with maturity, ego development, in the absence of well-being, also probably falls short. The complex ego, overwhelmed by conflict and ambivalence or left disillusioned by life's difficult lessons, misses central aspects of maturity such as self-acceptance and contentment. True maturity incorporates both the complex sensibility implied by ego development as well as the context of positive feelings and resilience implied by well-being. If we consider these two facets of maturity as important indicators of adult development, we might ask how a person accomplishes each, an issue we now consider.

Block (1982) described how Piaget's concepts of assimilation and accommodation may characterize personality development. In assimilation, existing cognitive structures are used to make sense out of the current environment. Assimilation allows a person to enjoy a sense of meaning because life experiences fit into his or her preexisting meaning structures. Thus, assimilation and its affective consequences may reinforce one's approach to life and ultimately contribute to well-being.

Of course, life does not always conform to our expectations. *Accommodation* refers to the process of modifying existing cognitive structures when life requires a central change in the self. While assimilation promotes stability and a ready sense of meaning, accommodation entails disruption and the active search for meaning in life experiences. Research has shown that ego development relates to the experience of life difficulties and the active struggle to make sense out of experience that is captured by the concept of accommodation (King, Scollon, Ramsey, and Williams, 2000). In considering the relationship between ego development and experience, we suggest that a lens may be an appropriate metaphor. The relatively less developed ego sees the world "through a glass, darkly"—in simple ways, missing the nuances that a sharper focus might provide. Experiences confront the person, perhaps beveling the lens in particular ways, allowing aspects of reality to come into sharper focus. When we are faced with significant life events, we have the opportunity to develop the complexity of our perspectives and, ultimately, our selves (King and Hicks, 2006). With regard to ego development, one might say, "What doesn't kill me, makes me more complex."

In sum, our approach to maturity encompasses two independent aspects of adulthood: one associated with a sense of positive well-being, fulfillment, and assured meaning, and the other encompassing difficulty, complexity, and openness. How do these two aspects of maturity relate to lost and found possible selves—to the adult's capacity to acknowledge what might have been, while also investing in a new set of goals commensurate with what has been lost?

Lost Possible Selves: The Place of What Might Have Been in Maturity

Lost possible selves are similar to regrets, and given the robust negative relationship between regrets and well-being (Stewart and Vandewater, 1999; Torges, Stewart, and Miner-Rubino, 2005; Wrosch, Bauer, and Scheier, 2005), it is perhaps not surprising that the salience of a lost possible self has been associated with lowered well-being, heightened distress, and increased regret (King and Raspin, 2004). In other words, reporting that one thinks a great deal about a goal that is no longer available is associated with misery—for both divorced women and gay men and lesbians (King and Raspin, 2004; King and Smith, 2004). Thinking about lost goals is simply no way to be happy.

New Directions for Adult and Continuing Education • DOI: 10.1002/ace

Happiness requires that individuals truly divest themselves of previously sought goals, but ego development—the capacity to experience the world and oneself in complex, sophisticated ways—may require an examination of these very goals. Among divorced women, lost possible self elaboration (not salience) related to current ego development in interaction with time since divorce (King and Raspin, 2004). Note the importance of time in these results. For women who had only recently divorced, a highly elaborate lost possible self might simply demonstrate good memory for recently lost goals. Importantly, then, lost possible self elaboration was related to higher levels of concurrent ego development only in interaction with time. Among these women, ego development related specifically to narrating a long-lost aspect of the self with rich, vivid detail. Furthermore, lost self elaboration predicted enhanced ego development, in interaction with time, prospectively, over two years (King and Raspin, 2004). Similarly, among gay men and lesbians, elaborating on a straight possible self was associated with concurrent ego development, as well as increased ego development two years later, even after controlling for a variety of potential confounds (King and Smith, 2004).

Elaborating on one's lost goals suggests a tolerance for one's own vulnerability, an acknowledgment of change, and a lack of defensiveness in the face of one's inconsistencies—qualities that may be characteristics of the developed and developing person. Lost goals appear to relate in complex ways to maturity. Thinking about these goals is a source of distress, but the ability to generate a rich portrait of a previously cherished goal is associated with complexity of one's view of the world along with increasing complexity over time. Although thinking about loss may be uncomfortable, bringing up regret and even embarrassment over one's previous naiveté, this task predicts enhanced development over time. Thus, lost possible self-exploration may represent a trade-off: the temporary sacrifice of good feelings in the service of enhanced understanding. In addition to confronting and perhaps eventually resolving one's past, we have suggested that a person must recommit to a new set of goals that are commensurate with his or her lost incentives. What are the implications of these new goals for maturity?

Found Possible Selves: The Place of What Might Still Be

Generally pursuing and progressing on important goals is associated with enhanced well-being (Little, 1999). Thus, it is not surprising that the salience of current best possible selves is related to well-being (for the divorced women, King and Raspin, 2004; as well as parents of children with Down syndrome, King and Patterson, 2000; and gay men and lesbians, King and Smith, 2004). These results converge with a broad array of studies to suggest that investing in one's current goals is a strong correlate of well-being. In addition, among women who have experienced divorce, the elaboration of

New Directions for Adult and Continuing Education • DOI: 10.1002/ace

the found possible self was related to enhanced well-being (King and Raspin, 2004). Recall that for many of these women, the experience of divorce was extraordinarily discombobulating. For these women, generating a rich, vivid set of new goals was strongly related to well-being. These results resonate with the idea that the past must be left behind while moving on to enjoy a satisfying life.

Results with regard to lost and found possible selves suggest a paradox of maturity. While fully investing oneself in the present and future is associated with happiness, the capacity to acknowledge a nuanced and elaborate lost possible self is related to development and predicts continued development over time. These results suggest the dynamic interplay of happiness and complexity, assimilation and accommodation, over time. Well-being is associated with commitment to current goals and focus on the good that is yet to come. Ego development is related to the capacity to acknowledge loss and expound on one's previously cherished goals. True maturity may be the convergence of happiness and complexity, suggesting that when they exist side by side, these two qualities produce a unique synthesis of wisdom and acknowledged loss, on the one hand, and hope and optimism for the future, on the other.

The Satisfaction with Life Scale (Diener, Emmons, Larsen, and Griffin, 1985) is a commonly used measure of well-being, which has been used in all of the studies described here. One item on that scale is particularly worth considering at this point: "If I could live my life over, I would change almost nothing." This item gets straight to the heart of the question of the role of loss in adulthood. For the person who is high on ego development, a score of 7 means endorsing the value of one's life, "warts and all"—even given that that life has included experiences that might be considered traumatic, difficult, and even unfathomable to an outsider. In the transformational light of accommodation, regrets are realistically negative, but they become less regrettable as they are incorporated into the ever changing life story. In the context of an elaborated lost possible self, we might acknowledge that that score of 7 comes not from complacency or denial but is indeed a true accomplishment.

Implications for Adult Education: Looking Back, Coming Back, and Moving Forward

Whether a person is coming back to school, finishing an unmet goal from the past, or seeking to enhance life's interest by returning to school, we can note that all adults are poised to become, even as their current goals exist in a context of previous possible selves and forsaken life dreams. Often a person may, like the women in our study, have been caught off guard by life experience. Many of these women would admit to being humbled by life, but it is worth noting that unmet expectations may be a key to development.

Even as our previous expectations reveal our naiveté and foolhardiness, examination of these expectations, though painful, may result in a richer, more complex self.

A large body of evidence suggests that investing in goals is an important aspect of well-being throughout life (see Cantor and Sanderson, 1999). But investing in goals may be a risky proposition, fraught with potential for failure and ultimately regret. Yet note that accommodation cannot occur if a person is not invested in his or her preexisting meaning structures. Thus, goal investment, though potentially making the person vulnerable to distress in response to failure, may also be seen as predisposing the person toward growth in response to failure.

It has been said that only when the environment fails to meet one's expectations can real development occur (Loevinger, 1976). Implicit in this assertion is the experience of surprise. The capacity to admit to being surprised by life would appear to be essential to personality development in adulthood. Surprise requires that one admit to not knowing everything, not thinking of every possible contingency—in short, to being human. Perhaps underlying the capacity for surprise is a sense of humility (Exline and Geyer, 2004). Actively accommodating life experiences requires an admission of one's own vulnerability, the inadequacy of one's preexisting meaning structures in the face of the challenges of reality, and one's apparent smallness in the grand scheme of life.

In a sense, both aspects of maturity require courage. Admission that one had perhaps foolishly embraced an untenable future self is threatening. Confronting loss, sacrificing happiness, and undertaking the difficult process of self-examination would appear to require fortitude. But exploration of loss is not the sole predictor of maturity. The individual must also have commitments to current goals. Starting anew—dedicating oneself to commitments after loss, having the capacity to expect something from life, even after one's prior expectations have failed—requires courage. Indeed, the capacity to commit to goals within the context of having experienced goal loss may be the best expression of maturity.

Life's disappointments and calamities may make one well aware of the folly of planning or the potentially disastrous consequences of hoping. The mature person is one who maintains the central notion that life does matter and that there is meaning in attachment to the events of the world. Even forsaken goals serve as markers of values and beliefs about the self and world. The mature person reveals the capacity to recognize and even celebrate those relics of an earlier self—a more naive self, to be sure, but one who might nevertheless be lauded for her optimism, enthusiasm, and innocence. The capacity to courageously invest in one's current life dream, while simultaneously confronting the vivid recollection of a lost life dream, speaks to the resilience of the happy person as well as the complex, open, and humane orientation to the world that is ego development.

References

Block, J. "Assimilation, Accommodation, and the Dynamics of Personality Development." *Child Development,* 1982, *53,* 281–295.

Cantor, N., and Sanderson, C. A. "Life Task Participation and Wellbeing: The Importance of Taking Part in Daily Life." In D. Kahneman, E. Diener, and N. Schwarz (eds.), *Well-Being: The Foundations of Hedonic Psychology.* New York: Russell Sage Foundation, 1999.

Cross, S., and Markus, H. "Possible Selves Across the Life Span." *Human Development,* 1991, *34,* 230–255.

Diener, E., Emmons, R. A., Larsen, R. J., and Griffin, S. "The Satisfaction with Life Scale." *Journal of Personality Assessment,* 1985, *49,* 71–75.

Emmons, R. A., Colby, P. M., and Kaiser, H. A. "When Losses Lead to Gains: Personal Goals and the Recovery of Meaning." In P.T.P. Wong and P. S. Fry (eds.), *The Human Quest for Meaning: A Handbook of Psychological Research and Clinical Applications.* Mahwah, N.J.: Erlbaum, 1998.

Exline, J. J., and Geyer, A. L. "Perceptions of Humility & Preliminary Study." *Self and Identity,* 2004, *3,* 95–114.

Helson, R., and Wink, P. "Two Conceptions of Maturity Examined in the Findings of a Longitudinal Study." *Journal of Personality and Social Psychology,* 1987, *53,* 531–541.

Hy, I X, and Loevinger, J. *Measuring Ego Development.* (2nd ed.) Mahwah, N.J.: Erlbaum, 1996.

King, L. A. "Who Is Regulating What and Why? The Motivational Context of Self-Regulation." *Psychological Inquiry,* 1996, *7,* 57–61.

King, L. A. "Personal Goals and Personal Agency: Linking Everyday Goals to Future Images of the Self." In M. Kofta, G. Weary, and G. Sedek (eds.), *Personal Control in Action: Cognitive and Motivational Mechanisms.* New York City: Plenum, 1998.

King, L. A. "The Hard Road to the Good Life: The Happy, Mature Person." *Journal of Humanistic Psychology,* 2001, *41,* 51–72.

King, L. A. "Personal Goals and Life Dreams: Positive Psychology and Motivation in Daily Life." In W. Gardner and J. Shah (eds.), *Handbook of Motivation Science.* New York: Guilford Press, forthcoming.

King, L. A., and Hicks, J. A. "Narrating the Self in the Past and the Future: Implications for Maturity." *Research in Human Development,* 2006, *3,* 121–138.

King, L. A., and Patterson, C. "Reconstructing Life Goals After the Birth of a Child with Down Syndrome: Finding Happiness and Growing." *International Journal of Rehabilitation and Health,* 2000, *5,* 17–30.

King, L. A., and Raspin, C. "Lost and Found Possible Selves, Subjective Well-Being, and Ego Development in Divorced Women." *Journal of Personality,* 2004, *72,* 603–632.

King, L. A., Scollon, C. K., Ramsey, C. M., and Williams, T. "Stories of Life Transition: Happy Endings, Subjective Well-Being, and Ego Development in Parents of Children with Down Syndrome." *Journal of Research in Personality,* 2000, *34,* 509–536.

King, L. A., and Smith, N. G. "Gay and Straight Possible Selves: Goals, Identity, Subjective Well-Being, and Personality Development." *Journal of Personality,* 2004, *75,* 967–994.

Little, B. R. "Personality and Motivation: Personal Action and the Conative Evolution." In L. Pervin and J. P. Oliver (eds.), *Handbook of Personality: Theory and Research.* (2nd ed.) New York: Guilford Press, 1999.

Loevinger, J. *Ego Development: Conceptions and Theories.* San Francisco: Jossey-Bass, 1976.

Loevinger, J. "Completing a Sentence." In P. M. Wesatenberg, A. Blasi, and L. D. Cohn (eds.), *Personality Development.* Mahwah, N.J.: Erlbaum, 1998.

Markus, H., and Nurius, P. "Possible Selves." *American Psychologist,* 1986, *41,* 954–969.

McCrae, R. R., and Costa, P. T. "Openness to Experience and Ego Level in Loevinger's Sentence Completion Test: Dispositional Contributions to Developmental Models of Personality." *Journal of Personality and Social Psychology,* 1980, *39,* 1179–1190.

Mroczek, D. K. "Age and Emotion in Adulthood." *Current Directions in Psychological Science,* 2001, *10,* 87–90.

Mroczek, D. K., and Spiro, A. "Change in Life Satisfaction During Adulthood: Findings from the Veterans Affairs Normative Aging Study." *Journal of Personality and Social Psychology,* 2005, *88,* 189–202.

Noam, G. I. "Solving the Ego Development-Mental Health Riddle." In A. Blasi and P. Westenberg (eds.), *Personality Development: Theoretical, Empirical, and Clinical Investigations of Loevinger's Conception of Ego Development.* Mahwah, N.J.: Erlbaum, 1998.

Pals, J. L., and John, O. P. "How Are Dimensions of Adult Personality Related to Ego Development? An Application of the Typological Approach." In P. M. Westenberg, A. Blasi, and L. D. Cohn (eds.), *Personality Development: Theoretical, Empirical, and Clinical Investigations of Loevinger's Conception of Ego Development.* Mahwah, N.J.: Erlbaum, 1998.

Ruvolo, A. P., and Markus, H. R. "Possible Selves and Performance: The Power of Self-Relevant Imagery." *Social Cognition,* 1992, *10,* 95–124.

Sheldon, K. M., and Kasser, T. "Goals, Congruence, and Positive Well-Being: New Empirical Support for Humanistic Theories." *Journal of Humanistic Psychology,* 2001, *41,* 30–50.

Stewart, A. J., and Vandewater, E. A. "'If I Had It to Do Over Again . . .': Midlife Review, Midcourse Corrections, and Women's Well-Being in Midlife." *Journal of Personality and Social Psychology,* 1999, *76,* 270–283.

Torges, C. M., Stewart, A. J., and Miner-Rubino, K. "Personality After the Prime of Life: Men and Women Coming to Terms with Regrets." *Journal of Research in Personality,* 2005, *39,* 148–165.

Westen, D. "Loevinger's Theory of Ego Development in the Context of Contemporary Psychoanalytical Theory." In P. M. Westebberg, A. Blasi, and L. D. Cohn (eds.), *Personality Development: Theoretical, Empirical and Clinical Investigations of Loevinger's Conception of Ego Development.* Mahwah, N.J.: Erlbaum, 1998.

Wrosch, C., Bauer, I., and Scheier, M. F. (2005) Regret and Quality of Life Across the Adult Life Span: The Influence of Disengagement and Available Future Goals. *Psychology and Aging, 20,* 657–670.

LAURA A. KING is professor of psychological sciences at the University of Missouri, Columbia, and editor-in-chief of the Journal of Research in Personality.

JOSHUA A. HICKS is a doctoral student at the University of Missouri, Columbia, with interests in personality development and the experience of meaning in life.

4

This chapter describes the educational possible selves of low-income mothers as they make the transition from welfare to work.

Reaching for the Future: The Education-Focused Possible Selves of Low-Income Mothers

Shawna J. Lee, Daphna Oyserman

More individuals than ever before are pursuing higher education to prepare themselves for a competitive labor market. This may mean returning to the classroom to attain a general equivalency diploma (GED) degree, or going on to technical college, community college, or a four-year university to attain job training and skills. Studies show that those who attain a GED have higher earnings than high school dropouts (Boesel, Alsalam, and Smith, 1998), and data are strongly supportive of the link between increased education at all levels and higher earnings. For example, in 2004, the median weekly earnings for full-time female workers with an associate degree was $608, compared to $488 for women with only a high school diploma (U.S. Bureau of the Census, 2005). As a result, an increasing number of nontraditional students are returning to the classroom. Based on the National Households Education Survey of 2001, participation in adult education increased from 40 percent in 1995 to 46 percent in 2001, with more women than men seeking adult education (Kim, Hagedorn, Williamson, and Chapman, 2004). This increase in nontraditional students suggests that individuals are pursuing their educational and employment goals well into adulthood, perhaps with the desire to use education as a means to achieve employment and financial gains.

While this is a promising trend, some segments of society may still be left behind. In this chapter we focus on low-income mothers who are making

NEW DIRECTIONS FOR ADULT AND CONTINUING EDUCATION, no. 114, Summer 2007 © 2007 Wiley Periodicals, Inc.
Published online in Wiley InterScience (www.interscience.wiley.com) • DOI: 10.1002/ace.255

the transition from welfare to work. These mothers often have low levels of education and few job skills (Danziger, Ananat, and Browning, 2000). The jobs they are able to find tend to be concentrated in low-wage occupations (Lee, 2004; Loprest, 1999), and even with years of work experience, many former welfare recipients do not attain jobs with wages above the official U.S. poverty level (Danziger and Johnson, 2005; Loprest and Zedlewski, 2006). Low-income mothers in the transition from welfare to work face barriers that may deter their educational pursuits; the demands of caregiving and employment leave little time for education, and attaining an education is expressly not a goal of the welfare system. Yet education is central to job mobility. Studies show that job retention is difficult for women moving out of welfare in part because of lack of education, little past work experience, and deficits in soft skills such as work attitudes (Holzer and Wissoker, 2001; Loprest and Zedlewski, 2006). Facilitating the pursuit of educational goals may be one way to improve long-term outcomes for current and former welfare recipients who are moving to the workforce.

Possible Selves and How They Are Related to Behavior

Possible selves are the future-oriented aspect of identity, or the selves that one expects to become as well as the selves one wishes to avoid becoming (Markus and Nurius, 1986). Possible selves may be rooted in past successes and failures, and they also provide a way to make sense of one's current situation (Cross and Markus, 1991). For example, thinking about a future possible self of attending college is one way to understand behaviors enacted in the present that are related to that goal, such as studying hard and attending class. Possible selves can also facilitate identity exploration; that is, they are one way to try on new ideas about who you are and who you will become (Dunkel and Anthis, 2001). Among adults, new possible selves may emerge from a change in life phase or social context (Frazier and Hooker, 2006). For example, the life transition of becoming a parent increases the salience of parenting-focused possible selves (Hooker and others, 1996). Similarly, changes in welfare policy forcing transition to work result in greater salience of breadwinner possible selves among women who might otherwise focus primarily on parenting and family-focused possible selves (Lee and Oyserman, 2006).

In addition to representing positive images of the self one expects to become, possible selves include concerns for the future and the self-images one fears or wishes to avoid becoming. Feared possible selves in the academic domain may include wishing to avoid failing out of school or getting bad grades (Oyserman, Bybee, and Terry, 2006). Balance in possible selves—that is, when feared possible selves are paired with positive expected possible selves—is known to have important motivational consequences (Oyserman, Bybee, and Terry, 2006; Oyserman, Bybee, Terry, and Hart-Johnson, 2004).

New Directions for Adult and Continuing Education • DOI: 10.1002/ace

Balanced possible selves promotes attainment because linking a positive expected self to a feared self in the same domain pinpoints motivation to both work toward a positive future goal and to anticipate and strategize how to get around problems that may result in ending as a failure in that domain (one's feared possible self) (Oyserman, Bybee, Terry, and Hart-Johnson, 2004). The need for balance may be especially significant in low-income contexts because it is important to anticipate and plan for set-backs when barriers to education attainment are more likely to be present. It is not enough to expect to do well; one also has to be worried about doing badly.

Possible selves can create the link between hopes and dreams and current action by connecting behaviors with future desired selves (Cross and Markus, 1991; Lee and Oyserman, 2006; Oyserman and Markus, 1990). Seeing how behaviors are linked with distal goals like having a career can be difficult. To address this difficulty, it is necessary to feel that the distal possible self of a career is linked with more proximal possible selves like joining an adult education program. The act of connecting distal and proximal goals increases the importance of engaging in behaviors such as signing up for classes, attending class, and doing homework. This link between distal and proximal possible selves provides the pathway between the present and future goals. Intervention may facilitate efforts to link possible selves and current action. For example, the School-to-Jobs program successfully connected possible selves to current action, and students consequently demonstrated improved grades, reduced absences, improved in-class behavior, and fewer depressive symptoms at two-year follow-up (Oyserman, Bybee, and Terry, 2006; Oyserman, Terry, and Bybee, 2002).

The Educational Goals of Adult Women

Research linking possible selves to education has primarily been conducted with adolescents. These studies point out that education is important to low-income minority youth, despite a gap between desired possible selves (for example, going to college, becoming a doctor) and current educational attainment (Oyserman and Fryberg, 2006; Yowell, 2002). Yet to date, little is known about the educational possible selves of low-income mothers. A basic supposition of possible selves theory is that the array of possible selves one has at a particular time shapes what is believed to be possible for the future (Oyserman, forthcoming). Research demonstrates that family- and parenting-focused possible selves are important to women (Hooker and others, 1996; Lee and Oyserman, 2006); it is not known whether women focusing on the need to enter the workforce envision education-related possible selves as a part of that process. Moreover, it is not clear whether educational goals fit with other important possible selves related to parenting and employment (Kerpelman, Shoffner, and Ross-Griffin, 2002).

Examining the Education-Focused Possible Selves of Low-Income Mothers

To address these questions, we examine the education-focused possible selves of two groups of low-income mothers: women who were applying for welfare benefits at a Department of Human Service (DHS) welfare office and women currently participating in a mandated welfare-to-work job training program (JTP). Possible selves were generated in response to an open-ended measure and then content-coded. First, we present data on the frequency of various possible selves that respondents listed, separating expected possible selves from feared possible selves and examining the strategies women describe as being linked to working on attaining possible selves or avoiding becoming like their feared possible selves. We test the hypothesis that women in the job training setting are less focused on educational goals than those applying for welfare benefits because women in job training are pressed to focus on breadwinning, while those who are still eligible for benefits can focus on education, perhaps as a means of becoming economically self-sufficient at a later time.

Participants were 313 mothers who were on average thirty-one years old (range: eighteen to fifty-nine years). About half of women ($n = 171$) were recruited from Michigan JTPs and the other half ($n = 142$) from DHS welfare office waiting rooms. Women were participating in job training programs to meet welfare-to-work requirements but were located separately from the welfare office. DHS participants were applying for benefits or visiting a caseworker. All of the women had at least one child living at home, and most (64 percent) were caring for children under the age of five. About four in ten participants were working at least part time (41 percent of DHS mothers and 42 percent of job training mothers). About half of the women (51.2 percent) were African American, others were mostly European American (40.6 percent), and the remaining 8.25 percent of mothers of another ethnic background. Though four in ten (40 percent) of mothers reported some education beyond high school, most had no education beyond that: 22 percent had not finished high school, 17 percent had a GED, and 21 percent had a high school diploma.

To assess possible selves, mothers were asked to describe their possible selves for the coming year with open-ended questions ("Next year, I expect to be . . ." and "Next year I want to avoid being . . ."). They were also asked what strategies, if any, they were using to reach their possible selves. Responses were content-coded as to whether they focused on the categories that follow, with illustrative examples for each category provided:

- Jobs—for example: getting a full-time job, working for myself, getting a stable job
- Material concerns—for example: having a car, moving into a better apartment, buying clothes for children

- Education—for example: going to school to be a nurse's assistant, getting job training
- Caregiving—for example: helping at my child's school more, making sure children stay out of trouble, worrying about family members
- Mental health—for example: not being depressed, being happy, trying to maintain a positive outlook
- Physical health—for example: expecting to lose weight, fearing substance abuse, or staying off drugs

Job and material concerns were most prevalent, with 73 percent of the respondents mentioning at least one job-expected possible self and 60 percent mentioning at least one expected-material-concern possible self. Yet education was highly salient: 39 percent of the respondents generated at least one expected education-related possible self, and 29 percent reported at least one strategy to attain that educational possible self. Because the focus of this chapter is education, results related to other domains are discussed in more detail elsewhere (Lee and Oyserman, 2006).

Employment (35 percent) and material concerns (43 percent) were also the most prevalent feared possible selves. In all domains, respondents reported far fewer feared possible selves than expected possible selves. Although all respondents generated at least one expected possible self, 91 percent generated at least one feared possible self. Respondents averaged 2.90 expected possible selves and 2.29 feared possible selves. Feared educational possible selves followed this pattern, with only 9 percent of respondents indicating that there were any education-related fears that they wished to avoid in the next year.

Descriptive Content of Expected Possible Selves. Content analysis of possible selves revealed the major concerns of the low-income mothers in this study. When educational goals were mentioned as an expected possible self, they were often broad and frequently included a general expectation such as obtaining a GED or going back to college.

However, many respondents explicitly linked education with their employment possible selves. Education was seen as a way to attain a career and find more satisfying employment, for example, linking the expectation of "being a manager" with the strategy of "learning and going to school." Education was even more common as a strategy to attain specific employment goals, such as working in day care, medical billing, or accounting, or being an emergency medical technician, mortgage broker, or home health care aide. For example, the expected possible self of being a day care provider was connected to the strategy of "becoming certified," or "working as an EMT" paired with the strategy of "finishing my course work." In sum, women's employment goals were seen through the lens of education, and pursuing education was second only to "going out there to apply for jobs" as a strategy for attaining better employment.

Although few respondents were in school, those who were generated expected possible selves such as getting better grades, working on taking a proficiency exam, or waiting for the results of an exam. For those expecting to return to school, obtaining financial resources for education was the most commonly mentioned strategy to attain education-related possible selves. For example, the possible self of expecting to return to school was paired with strategies such as applying for financial aid, trying to get other sources of funding, paying off debts, waiting for transcripts to arrive from out of state, and getting registered for classes.

Importantly, education was connected to women's caregiving roles. A number of the mothers wrote about education in terms of their expectations for their children's educational futures. Emblematic of this were expected possible selves of "my child finishing high school," "my kids to be in the best school," or "sending my kids to college." Though not explicitly related to their personal educational expectations, education was seen as a way to care for children—for example, by expecting to be "volunteering more at my son's school" or "being involved more in my son's school activities."

Content of Feared Possible Selves.   Overall, women generated fewer feared possible selves. Perhaps because relatively few were currently in school, education-related feared possible selves were uncommon. However, for those who were in school, responses included wanting to avoid "failing school" paired with the strategy of "working hard to stay on top of my grades," or wanting to avoid being "a failure in school" paired with the strategy of "getting things done early." Noteworthy is that at least one respondent who indicated wanting to avoid being on welfare in the next year linked that possible self with the specific strategy of "going to college."

Regression Analyses.   Regression analyses were conducted to examine if individuals in the job training sites and welfare offices differed in the extent to which they were focused on education possible selves, with the hypothesis that being under immediate pressure to find employment (such as for women in the job training site) would be negatively related to frequency of education-related possible selves. (Negative binomial regression was used because the possible selves in the education domain were measured as a count score—total number of education-related possible selves mentioned—and data were skewed toward zero. Negative binomial regression is a maximum-likelihood Poisson model that is appropriate when the independent variable consists of nonnegative integer count of relatively uncommon events, such as criminal offenses; Osgood, 2000.)

Regression analyses indicated that there were no significant differences among women in the frequency of education-related possible selves. After controlling for education, race, current employment, and the number of children currently living at home, women in the job training programs and those applying for welfare were equally likely to have expected ($\beta = -.26$, $p = .24$), feared ($\beta = -.13, p = .79$), and developed strategies ($\beta = -.17$, $p = .46$) related to their education possible selves.

Emerging Themes

There are a number of reasons that it is important to examine the possible selves of adult women. As Frazier and Hooker (2006) noted, possible selves are a theoretical construct that can provide a blueprint for understanding unique aspects of self-development and the evolution of self-concept in adulthood. Possible selves serve as one way to understand the structure of one's current and future self (Cross and Markus, 1991; Leonardi, Syngolli-tou, and Kiosseoglou, 1998; Markus and Nurius, 1986). We extend the theory of possible selves to investigate the educational expectations of low-income mothers. Using possible selves theory will help educators and policymakers facilitate the transition from welfare to work by providing a fuller understanding of effective strategies to surmount the barriers that low-income mothers face in attaining their goals.

Content analysis and regression results indicated that employment and material concerns were a pressing reality for the low-income mothers in this study. Although research indicates that women in job training sites are more focused on employment than their counterparts applying for welfare benefits (Lee and Oyserman, 2006), respondents in this study did not differ in terms of their focus on education. A surprisingly large percentage (38 percent) of the respondents mentioned at least one expected possible self related to education. All of the respondents were mothers, and nearly half of the respondents were also currently working, yet higher education was a highly salient future self for the respondents and was also mentioned as an aspiration for their children. However, pursuit of education in itself was not the end goal for most of these women. Only a small number mentioned the desire to gain knowledge simply for the sake of learning or personal growth. Most responses suggested that the women in this study see education as a means to achieve a better way of life by improving their employment options. The notion that education is a way off welfare and out of poverty is recurrent in women's educational possible selves (Lee and Oyserman, 2006; Oyserman and Fryberg, 2006).

Although many respondents have expected possible selves focused on education, few had feared educational possible selves. These results parallel several other studies indicating that feared possible selves are less salient (Leondari, Syngollitou, and Kiosseoglou, 1998; Robinson and Davis, 2003; Yowell, 2002). Yowell's study of Hispanic adolescent youth (2002) indicated that while many youth viewed education as a highly salient expectation for the future, fewer had feared possible selves or educational possible selves. Similarly, two studies of low-income women indicate that respondents had fewer feared than expected occupational possible selves (Lee and Oyserman, 2006; Robinson and Davis, 2003).

This dearth of feared possible selves means that women are less likely to have balanced education-focused possible selves. While focusing on the positive may seem like a good strategy, visualizing only positive outcomes without visualizing possible failure and strategizing how to get around it is not likely to be sufficient to sustain the motivation of low-income mothers to attain education-focused possible selves in the face of the real obstacles to time, energy, and resources they face. Balance may be especially important in a low-income context where obstacles and barriers to attaining possible selves are likely to present themselves, thus necessitating the need to anticipate and plan for setbacks. Indeed, targeting balance in possible selves and increasing the feasibility of possible selves strategies is one of the key reasons that past interventions have been successful in improving the academic and mental health outcomes of low-income minority youth (Oyserman and others, 2004; Oyserman, Johnson, and Bybee, 2005; Oyserman, Terry, and Bybee, 2002). Thus, lack of feared education possible selves may be a risk factor indicating that low-income mothers in the transition from welfare to work do not have the self-regulatory focus that would promote attainment of educational goals.

Implications for Intervention

It is difficult to turn possible selves into reality. Although women's educational possible selves clearly represent important and self-relevant goals, low-income mothers face a number of barriers, such as lack of adequate child care and transportation, that present challenges to educational pursuits (Danziger, Ananat, and Browning, 2004; Danziger and others, 2000). Furthermore, education is inconsistent with the welfare reform policy work-first model that is focused on reducing the welfare roles by attaching women to the labor market as quickly as possible. Thus, intervention to help women attain their employment and educational possible selves is warranted at multiple points.

First, there is a need for welfare reform policies to support the educational goals of low-income mothers. Although the work-first model of quick attachment to the labor market may be beneficial in terms of reducing welfare caseloads in the short term, job retention is hindered by lack of adequate training and poor attitudes about working (Holzer and Wissoker, 2001). Educational attainment may be an effective long-term job training tool within the welfare system. Such activities could augment existing work-first activities, for example, by promoting vocational training specific to the sorts of jobs women would like to attain (for example, vocational training focused on common job goals such as emergency medical technician, nurse practitioner, or day care licensure). Related to this, an additional policy change is to expand the list of education-related activities that count toward welfare-to-work requirements (Holzer and Wissoker, 2001).

Second, there is a need for individual-level interventions that link educational possible selves with activities to be enacted in the present. Using the example of education-related possible selves, one must first develop and then be able (Leondari, Syngollitou, and Kiosseoglou, 1998) to access those educational possible selves. Intervention should then focus on articulation of both expected (such as expecting to attain a GED) and feared possible selves (such as wishing to avoid not being considered for a job because of lack of a high school degree). A next step is to develop a concrete plan that links self-relevant expected and feared possible selves to behaviors in the present. Focus on facilitating women's personal employment goals may also promote better attitudes about work (Holzer and Wissoker, 2001). In the case of a low-income mother on welfare, developing a plan to sign up for GED classes or buying a study guide for the GED are present-oriented behaviors that can facilitate the possible self of attaining a GED.

A key component of possible selves intervention is promoting articulation of feasible strategies to attain possible selves. Strategies should be specific and attainable, and directly target barriers that research indicates women will encounter in the process of attaining education. These strategies may build on past successful experiences with employment and education, or use the experiences of close others who have been successful. For example, a positive role model such as a mother or sibling who has attained higher education may make goals seem more attainable (Kerpelman, Shoffner, and Ross-Griffin, 2002; Robinson and Davis, 2003).

Conclusion

In this study, we expanded current knowledge related to the possible selves of low-income mothers. We documented the high frequency of education-related possible selves and showed that mothers in job training site and other welfare settings are equally likely to have education-related possible selves. Welfare programs and policies would better serve women's long-term job interests if they addressed the educational possible selves of low-income mothers. This could be accomplished through innovative interventions that integrate policy-level initiatives supporting women's educational goals and individual-level intervention targeting articulation of feared educational possible selves and specific strategies intended to facilitate attainment of possible selves.

References

Boesel, D., Alsalam, N., and Smith, T. M. *Educational and Labor Market Performance of GED Recipients.* Washington, D.C.: U.S. Department of Education, 1998.

Cross, S., and Markus, H. "Possible Selves Across the Lifespan." *Human Development,* 1991, *34*, 230–255.

Danziger, S., and Johnson, R. C. "Welfare Reform: The Morning After." *Milken Institute Review,* 2005, *1*, 9–15.

Danziger, S. K., Ananat, E. O., and Browning, K. G. "Childcare Subsidies and the Transition from Welfare to Work." *Family Relations,* 2004, *53*, 219–228.

Danziger, S. K., and others. "Barriers to Employment of Welfare Recipients." In R. Cherry and W. M. Rodgers III (eds.), *Prosperity for All? The Economic Boom and African Americans.* New York: Russell Sage Foundation, 2000.

Dunkel, C. S., and Anthis, K. S. "The Role of Possible Selves in Identity Formation: A Short-Term Longitudinal Study." *Journal of Adolescence,* 2001, *24,* 765–776.

Frazier, L. D., and Hooker, K. "Possible Selves in Adult Development: Linking Theory and Research." In C. Dunkel and J. Kerpelman (eds.), *Possible Selves: Theory, Research and Applications.* Happauge, N.Y.: Nova Science, 2006.

Holzer, H. J., and Wissoker, D. *How Can We Encourage Job Retention and Advancement for Welfare Recipients?* Washington, D.C.: Urban Institute, 2001.

Hooker, K., and others. "Possible Selves Among Parents of Infants and Preschoolers." *Developmental Psychology,* 1996, *32,* 542–550.

Kerpelman, J. L., Shoffner, M. F., and Ross-Griffin, S. "African American Mothers' and Daughters' Beliefs About Possible Selves and Their Strategies for Reaching the Adolescents' Future Academic and Career Goals." *Journal of Youth and Adolescence,* 2002, *31,* 289–302.

Kim, K., Hagedorn, M., Williamson, J., and Chapman, C. *Participation in Adult Education and Lifelong Learning: 2000–01.* Washington, D.C.: U.S. Department of Education, National Center for Education Statistics, 2004.

Lee, S. *Women's Work Supports, Job Retention, and Job Mobility: Child Care and Employer-Provided Health Insurance Help Women Stay on Jobs.* Washington, D.C.: Institute for Women's Policy Research, 2004.

Lee, S. J., and Oyserman, D. "Expecting to Work and Fearing Homelessness: The Possible Selves of Low-Income Women." Unpublished manuscript, 2006.

Leondari, A., Syngollitou, E., and Kiosseoglou, G. "Academic Achievement, Motivation and Possible Selves." *Journal of Adolescence,* 1998, *21,* 219–222.

Loprest, P. *How Families That Left Welfare Are Doing: A National Picture.* Washington, D.C.: Urban Institute, 1999.

Loprest, P., and Zedlewski, S. *The Changing Role of Welfare in the Lives of Low-Income Families with Children.* Washington, D.C.: Urban Institute, 2006.

Markus, H. R., and Nurius, P. "Possible Selves." *American Psychologist,* 1986, *41,* 954–969.

Osgood, D. W. "Poisson-Based Regression Analyses of Aggregate Crime Rates." *Journal of Quantitative Criminology,* 2000, *16*(1), 21–43.

Oyserman, D. "Social Identity and Self-Regulation." In E. T. Higgins and A. Kruglanski (eds.), *Social Psychology: Basic Principles.* (2nd ed.) New York: Guilford Press, forthcoming.

Oyserman, D., Bybee, D., and Terry, K. "Possible Selves and Academic Outcomes: How and When Possible Selves Impel Action." *Journal of Personality and Social Psychology,* 2006, *91,* 188–204.

Oyserman, D., Bybee, D., Terry, K., and Hart-Johnson, T. "Possible Selves as Roadmaps." *Journal of Research in Personality,* 2004, *38,* 130–149.

Oyserman, D., and Fryberg, S. "The Possible Selves of Diverse Adolescents: Content and Function Across Gender, Race and National Origin." In C. Dunkel and J. Kerpelman (eds.), *Possible Selves: Theory, Research, and Application.* Happauge, N.Y.: Nova Science, 2006.

Oyserman, D., Johnson, E., and Bybee, D. *Possible Selves in Early Adolescence: Content and Contextual Predictors.* Ann Arbor: University of Michigan, 2005.

Oyserman, D., and Markus, H. "Possible Selves in Balance: Implications for Delinquency." *Journal of Social Issues,* 1990, *46,* 141–157.

Oyserman, D., Terry, K., and Bybee, D. "A Possible Selves Intervention to Enhance School Involvement." *Journal of Adolescence,* 2002, *25,* 313–326.

Robinson, B. S., and Davis, K. L. "Motivational Attributes of Occupational Possible Selves for Low-Income Rural Women." *Journal of Counseling Psychology,* 2003, *50,* 156–164.

U.S. Bureau of the Census. *Women in the Labor Force: A Databook.* Washington, D.C.: U.S. Department of Labor, 2005.
Yowell, C. M. "Dreams of the Future: The Pursuit of Education and Career Possible Selves Among Ninth Grade Latino Youth." *Applied Developmental Science,* 2002, 6(2), 62–72.

SHAWNA J. LEE *is assistant professor in the School of Social Work at Wayne State University in Detroit, Michigan, and holds a joint appointment with the Merrill-Palmer Skillman Institute for Child and Family Development.*

DAPHNA OYSERMAN *is professor in the Department of Psychology and School of Social Work and research professor at the Institute for Social Research, University of Michigan, Ann Arbor.*

5

*This chapter discusses the ways in which societies'
gendered expectations may affect the possible selves
that women and men develop.*

Gender and Possible Selves

Hilary M. Lips

About twenty-five years ago, I had a conversation with a bright young
undergraduate student who was working as my research assistant at the
time. She was terrific on the computer—at a time when few students had
those skills—and I asked her why she had not decided to pursue a degree
in computer science or some related field. She said the computing she was
so good at and enjoyed so much just never seemed relevant to her career
and educational plans: it had never occurred to her to base any of her decisions on that particular talent.

That conversation echoed in my mind when I read a recent newspaper
article about the young actress Danica McKellar, who, though she is a well-
paid and well-recognized prime-time television star, offers high-level math
tutoring on her Web site just because she loves math. A math wiz, who as
an undergraduate helped to develop and prove a mathematical theorem that
bears her name, McKellar says that when she started as a freshman at UCLA,
she never considered majoring in math or science. "It wasn't like I thought
about it and thought, 'No, I can't do that,'" she is quoted as saying, 'It just
never occurred to me'" (Chang, 2005).

These stories speak volumes about the power of possible selves to
translate into life choices—and perhaps as well about the gendering of possible selves. These young women had not formed possible selves in the
realm of technology and science. They did not lack confidence in their abilities; they simply did not see themselves building educational or career
choices around those abilities. They had not formed possible selves as scientists or mathematicians. Why not? Probably in part because no one had
encouraged them to see themselves in that way, or had mentored them, or

NEW DIRECTIONS FOR ADULT AND CONTINUING EDUCATION, no. 114, Summer 2007 © 2007 Wiley Periodicals, Inc.
Published online in Wiley InterScience (www.interscience.wiley.com) • DOI: 10.1002/ace.256

had helped them take those talents seriously as the springboard to a variety of life choices. A young man with such flair for math or computing might more easily have found such encouragement, mentorship, and help.

Gender, Possible Selves, and Academic Choices

Women and men are still segregated into different occupations. In particular, there has been a marked underrepresentation of women in science and technology fields for many years, despite some increases in the number of women earning undergraduate and graduate degrees in science (National Science Foundation, 2004). The notion of possible selves can be applied broadly to the problem of why the tendency for young women and men to sort themselves (or at least allow themselves to be sorted) into different occupations is so persistent.

There is a great deal of research showing that students' current academic self-views affect the ways they experience their education, their performance, and the kinds of aspirations they emphasize. For example, among university students, seeing the self as mathematical or scientific has been found to predict performance on in-lab math tests, past math and science course enrollment, confidence with respect to career possibilities in math and science, intent to take more math and science courses, and the number of math and science courses actually taken for three years subsequent to the assessment (Lips, 1995). And the link between self-views and other academic variables is apparently gendered, at least within the realm of mathematics, science, and technology. For example, women college students, even those who have chosen math-intensive majors, have trouble associating math with their own selves if they implicitly stereotype mathematics as masculine (Nosek, Banaji, and Greenwald, 2002). Such research findings have been used to bolster the idea that educators should help young women feel more positive in their current self-views with respect to mathematics, science, and technology.

However, the underrepresentation of women in such fields may have as much to do with possible selves as with current self-views of ability. For example, some research indicates that even young women who have selected a university concentration in science or engineering lose their confidence in pursuing science and engineering careers as graduation nears (Hartman and Hartman, 2002; Ivie and Stowe, 2002). Are these young women revising their views of their own current abilities, or are they struggling with their visions of possible selves? They may find it increasingly difficult to picture themselves as engineers or scientists as the prospect of actually stepping into such roles confronts them. Or perhaps they do begin to picture themselves concretely in such careers—and the pictures are bleak. Female students in male-dominated areas anticipate more sex discrimination and think more about changing their major than do their counterparts in more traditional fields (Steele, James, and Barnett, 2002).

New Directions for Adult and Continuing Education • DOI: 10.1002/ace

Some research indicates that it is the possible selves rather than the current self-view that may diverge most sharply between young women and men as they approach graduation from university. For example, in one study of Canadian university students, a view of the self as inclined toward math or science predicted somewhat different things for female and male students. For men, a high self-rated inclination to mathematics and science predicted both a high self-rated likelihood of a math or science career and a high self-rated likelihood of a career in physical sciences or engineering. For women, a high self-rated inclination to mathematics and science predicted a high self-rated likelihood of a math or science career but not much self-rated likelihood of a career in physical sciences or engineering (Lips, 1993).

Studies of university students in the United States using the Lips Academic Self-View Survey (LASS) have assessed both how respondents view their current ability in and enjoyment of various academic areas and how they view the future possibilities for themselves as participants in further study in these areas. This research tends to show that female and male students are further apart in their perceptions of possible selves than in their views of their current selves. One study of university students, mainly juniors and seniors, revealed that males and females were fairly similar in their endorsement of current self views in both the math/science/business domain and the arts/culture/communication domain. However, when asked about future possibilities, the men indicated significantly greater likelihood than women that they would pursue the math/science/business domain, whereas the reverse was true for the arts/culture/communication domain (Lips, 2004). A second study that examined the same issues for high school students, university freshmen, and upper-level university students showed that for the women only, there was a significantly lower level of endorsement of possible selves in the math/science/business areas among university than high school students (Lips, 2004). It appears that as they progress to and through university, young women in the United States may revise their possible selves away from academic and career choices that involve the science and technology areas.

The gendering of possible selves in science and technology is not only a North American phenomenon. Research in New Zealand suggests that university students follow a pattern similar to that described above, with women and men diverging in their possible-self views more than in their current-self views. With respect to gender-related issues, data from New Zealand are of particular interest as a comparison to those of many other countries. New Zealand has a somewhat different history, tradition, and current reality than the United States does with respect to gender-related expectations. Women in New Zealand were the first in the world to get the vote. In recent years, both the prime minister of New Zealand and the leader of the parliamentary opposition have been women, as have been the governor general, the country's chief justice, and the CEO of the country's largest company. Women are rather well represented in parliament and in other powerful roles. As well, there has been a strong push in recent years to encourage women into scientific and technical fields, and the University of Auckland boasts that women make up some 20 to 25 percent of its engineering students—a higher percentage than any engineering school in the United States can claim.

LASS data collected from students enrolled in upper-level classes in engineering, business, computer science, and literature at two New Zealand universities showed, for the nonengineering students, that women and men were furthest apart on their self-descriptions of possible selves in the math/science/business domain and diverged less on current-self views (Lips, 2000a). The data do reveal, however, that women who choose engineering and remain on that path long enough to take senior-level courses have a different sense of their own strengths and possibilities than other college women do. Compared to the women in the rest of the sample, the female engineering students rated themselves more strongly in their current math- and science-related abilities and interests and in the possibility of pursuing further study in a cluster of areas (math, science, technology, business, and law) related to powerful careers. Indeed, they also produced current academic-self ratings that described themselves as better at and more strongly oriented toward mathematics and science than did their male fellow students in engineering. Nonetheless, even these women, although more confident than both their male and female counterparts in their current abilities in and fit to mathematics and science, showed a significantly lower tendency than male engineering students to forecast future possibilities for themselves that were consonant with powerful roles.

Clearly, then, possible selves are an important link in the chain of processes that lead women away from careers in natural science and technology. The research discussed here suggests that in understanding students' academic choices and futures, it is not enough to know how they view their current academic strengths and weaknesses. An understanding of the possibilities that students envision for themselves is critical in predicting, and perhaps influencing, the academic and career paths that they will follow.

Gender, Possible Selves, and Power

Women and men are segregated not only horizontally into different kinds of occupations but also vertically into differing levels of leadership in organizations. The shortage of women in leadership positions is a phenomenon that transcends national borders, industries, and occupations. For example, the boards of directors of U.S. companies listed in the Fortune Global 200 companies are only 17.5 percent female—and this is the *highest* percentage of any other country (Corporate Women Directors International, 2004). Only eight of the Fortune 500 companies can claim a female CEO (Jones, 2005). Women hold only 7.1 percent of the highest corporate officer titles and 14.4 percent of corporate officer positions in the Financial Post 500 in Canada (Catalyst, 2005). Women make up only 6.2 percent of CEOs and board chairs in South Africa (Businesswomen's Association and Catalyst, 2005).

Women political leaders are also scarce. A mere forty-six women served, some for very short terms, as prime ministers or presidents of countries during the twentieth century (Lewis, 2005). As of this writing, there are approximately twelve women in such roles. Women also lag behind men in positions of educational leadership: in 2001, more than 77 percent of the full professor positions at U.S. degree-granting institutions of higher education were men (National Center for Education Statistics, 2003). Women teachers are forty times less likely than their male counterparts to advance to the top leadership role of superintendent (Skrla, Reyes, and Scheurich, 2000).

One reason for the shortage of women at the top may be that young women are less likely than their male counterparts to imagine possible selves as holders of powerful roles. In one study (Lips, 2000b), university students were asked to imagine themselves first as "powerful persons" and then as holders of specific powerful roles: CEO of a major corporation, political leader, and director of a major scientific research center. For each role, the students were asked to provide a rating of how possible such a role was for them, how positive it would feel to hold such a role, and the specific things they expected to like and dislike about the role. The young women participating in this study reported less likelihood than the men did that they would ever hold one of these powerful roles, particularly the political leadership role.

Women also rated the political leadership role as less positive than the men did. The reasons for this rating became clear when we read their anticipated likes and dislikes with respect to their imagined roles. The women were more likely than the men to report anticipated relationship problems connected with leadership roles: many of them worried that these roles would make them too busy and stressed to have good family relationships and too disliked and feared by subordinates to have good relationships at work. Thus, even when forced to imagine a possible self as a political leader, it seems that many young women imagined a rather uncomfortable possible self—one to be avoided rather than pursued.

For men, the prospect of political leadership was more positive, and this gender difference highlights the ways in which the valence of possible selves can be influenced by divergent norms for femininity and masculinity. The exercise of some types of power and authority may feel antithetical to prescriptions for femininity; however, power and authority mesh nicely with prescriptions for masculinity. Women trying to envision powerful possible selves, then, may feel caught in a double bind: if they try to imagine themselves in certain powerful roles, they cannot escape the uncomfortable feeling that they would be either violating expectations for themselves as women (if they behave in strongly powerful ways) or that they would be unable to live up to the requirements of the powerful role (if they behave in stereotypically feminine ways). Some women may try to smooth over the contradictions by building stereotypically feminine values into their imagined roles. For example, women envisioning themselves as future leaders sometimes commented that in such roles, they would be able to help or protect others (Lips, 2001). It appears that women take into account society's contradictory prescriptions for powerful women when constructing visions of themselves as potential leaders.

Supporting the Development of New Possible Selves

Are there appropriate strategies for helping people to develop broader sets of possible selves? Some research on mentoring and modeling suggests there is. For example, research has shown that role models can inspire and guide students' academic aspirations (Hackett, 1985; Lockwood and Kunda, 1997), and even in the time-limited environment of the laboratory, the presence of competent female role models has a protective effect on young women's mathematics performance (Marx and Roman, 2002). It also shows that women who make it to graduate school in science fields identify encouragement from others as an important factor in their decisions (Hollenshead, Younce, and Wenzel, 1994).

One reason models and mentors may be so important is that people may resist or close off certain options because they believe that moving into those areas will entail fundamental changes in the way they are, the ways they view themselves, and the ways others view them—changes they do not want to make because they would then become atypical of their gender or unusual in some other way. In other words, becoming a political leader (or an engineer or a basic scientist) is seen not just as a matter of developing certain skills or competencies, but of developing a certain way of being and of viewing oneself and the world. This new way of being might be positive, but it can also be intimidating.

Here is where the often-noted lack of role models for women in fields such as politics, the physical sciences, computing, and engineering (and also the shortage of role models for men in fields such as nursing, child care, and elementary education) becomes especially poignant. If women and men thinking about pursuing gender-nontraditional fields could have a variety of role models of their own gender, the prospect of "turning into an engineer" or "turning into a first-grade school teacher" might not be so intimidating. The data bring us back to an original premise of the possible-selves concept: that we often form our possible selves through the observation of someone like us occupying a certain role.

Adult Education and Gendered Possible Selves

Education is often said to be potentially transformative, and adult education in particular is much discussed as an opportunity to alter one's fundamental view of oneself and the world. Indeed, according to transformative learning theory (Mezirow, 1991), education does not simply add knowledge or information; it also allows a shift in perspective and an expansion of one's sense of meaning and possibilities. This approach suggests that an adult's reentry into education can promote a series of reevaluative steps that lead to testing new options, searching for new meanings, and integrating these new meanings into a transformed perspective that includes a reevaluation of one's self-view. Such a self-reevaluation is likely to include some new possible selves.

Clearly, all education has the potential for changing students' sets of possible selves. This potential is especially likely to be realized in adult education, since many adult participants enroll in educational programs in response to personal transitions and changes (Aslanian, 2001). Adults may be spurred to enter college because of divorce, recent job loss, children leaving home, or the recognition that lack of credentials is impeding their chances of advancement in their careers (Kasworm, 2003). Individuals forced to respond to such life changes are likely to be aware that they need or want to modify the way they think about themselves and their possibilities, and they may well look to their educational experience to help them explore such changes in self-view. Alternatively, some adult students may return to education precisely because of revisions to their possible selves. These proactive planners hope to change careers because they no longer see themselves in the same way as they did when they first entered the labor force, and they can now envision different roles for themselves (Kasworm, 2003).

The idea of adult education as a vehicle for change in possible selves may be particularly relevant to women. Women are more frequent participants than men in adult education (Compton, Cox, and Laanan, 2006), and their numbers are rising more rapidly (Kasworm, 2003). They are also more likely than men to take adult education courses for personal interest (Kim, Hagedorn, Williamson, and Chapman, 2004). For women who have focused much of their energy on child rearing, even if they were also employed outside the home, adult education may be especially likely to provide an opportunity to reshape possible selves, expand horizons, and change long-held self-perceptions of ability and interest. Some of the programs that have developed to support women's return to school are rooted in an awareness of this opportunity. For example, Spelman College's Gateway program encourages women to think of themselves as potential leaders, the Education Development Center sponsors programs that help immigrant women envision themselves in a variety of nontraditional occupations, and Hollins University's Horizon program is designed to help women explore new options and new ways of seeing themselves and their abilities.

North American and other societies currently provide a social context in which traditional gendered roles for women and men are in flux. In recent decades, women have entered the labor force in large numbers, expectations for the division of domestic responsibilities within families have shifted somewhat (although the bulk of domestic work is still performed by women), and both men and women have opportunities to make choices about work and lifestyle that were not available to previous generations. Thus, changes in gender-related expectations form both a backdrop and fertile ground for the personal transformations that can be effected through education. As the research reviewed here suggests, such transformations are likely to be effected through the possible selves that students construct. Educators who wish to help students develop new self-relevant perspectives must focus not only on helping students become aware of their current strengths and abilities but also on helping them envision themselves in roles they have never before considered. Research indicates that one way of doing this is to expose students to role models—and in many cases, this will also involve being a role model or mentor.

References

Aslanian, C. B. *Adult Students Today*. New York: College Board, 2001.
Businesswomen's Association and Catalyst USA. *South African Women in Corporate Leaderships*. Census 2005. 2005. Retrieved July 15, 2006, from http://www.catalyst-women.org/headlines/files/2005%20Census%20of%20South%20African%20Women%20in%20Corporate%20Leadership.pdf.
Chang, K. "Between Series, an Actress Became a Superstar (in Math)." *New York Times*, July 19, 2005, p. D:22.
Compton, J. I., Cox, E., and Laanan, F. S. "Adult Learners in Transition." In F. S. Laanan (ed.), *Students in Transition: Trends and Issues*. New Directions for Student Services, no. 114. San Francisco: Jossey-Bass, 2006.
Corporate Women Directors International. "Women Board Directors of Fortune 200 Companies." 2004. Retrieved June 14, 2006, from http://www.globewomen.com/cwdi.
Hackett, G. "Role of Mathematics Self-Efficacy in the Choice of Math-Related Majors of College Women and Men: A Path Analysis." *Journal of Counseling Psychology*, 1985, 32, 47–56.
Hartman, H., and Hartman, M. "Comparing Female and Male Experiences in the Rowan Undergraduate Engineering Program." In *Women in a Knowledge-Based Society: Proceedings of the Twelfth International Congress on Women in Engineering and Science*. 2002. CD-ROM.
Hollenshead, C., Younce, P. S., and Wenzel, S. A. "Women Graduate Students in Mathematics and Physics: Reflections on Success." *Journal of Women and Minorities in Science and Engineering*, 1994, 1(1), 63–88.
Ivie, R., and Stowe, K. "U.S. Women in Academic Physics." *Women in a Knowledge-Based Society: Proceedings of the Twelfth International Congress on Women in Engineering and Science*. 2002. CD-ROM.
Jones, D. "Sara Lee Biggest Company (for Now) with Female CEO." *USA Today*, Feb. 11, 2005, p. B:4.
Kasworm, C. E. "Setting the Stage: Adults in Higher Education." In D. Kilgore and P. J. Rice (eds.), *Meeting the Needs of Adult Students*. New Directions for Student Services, no. 102. San Francisco, Jossey-Bass, 2003.
Kim, K., Hagedorn, M., Williamson, J., and Chapman, C. *Participation in Adult Education and Lifelong Learning: 2000-01*. Washington, D.C.: U.S. Government Printing Office, 2004.

Lewis, J. J. "About: Women's History." Womenshistory.about.com. July 22, 2005. Retrieved June 12, 2006, from http://womenshistory.about.com/library/weekly/aa010128a.htm.

Lips, H. M. "Bifurcation of a Common Path: Gender Splitting on the Road to Engineering and Physical Science Careers." *Initiatives*, 1993, *55*(3), 13–22.

Lips, H. M. "Through the Lens of Mathematical/Scientific Self-Schemas: Images of Students' Current and Possible Selves." *Journal of Applied Social Psychology*, 1995, *25*(19), 1671–1699.

Lips, H. M. "Gender and Ethnic Differences in Students' Academic Self-Views Among New Zealand University Students." Paper presented at the Twenty-Fifth International Congress of Psychology, Stockholm, Sweden, Aug. 2000a.

Lips, H. M. "College Students' Visions of Power and Possibility as Moderated by Gender." *Psychology of Women Quarterly*, 2000b, *24*(1), 39–43.

Lips, H. M. "Envisioning Positions of Leadership: The Expectations of University Students in Virginia and Puerto Rico." *Journal of Social Issues*, 2001, *57*, 799–813.

Lips, H. M. "The Gender Gap in Possible Selves: Divergence of Academic Self-Views Among High School and University Students." *Sex Roles*, 2004, *50*(5/6), 357–371.

Lockwood, P., and Kunda, Z. "Superstars and Me: Predicting the Impact of Role Models on the Self." *Journal of Personality and Social Psychology*, 1997, *73*, 91–103.

Marx, D. M., and Roman, J. S. "Female Role Models: Protecting Women's Math Test Performance." *Personality and Social Psychology Bulletin*, 2002, *28*(9), 1183–1193.

Mezirow, J. *Transformative Dimensions of Adult Learning.* San Francisco: Jossey-Bass, 1991.

National Center for Education Statistics. "Digest of Education Statistics, 2003, Table 231." *National Center for Education Statistics.* Washington, D.C.: Institute of Education Sciences, U.S.Department of Education, 2003. Retrieved June 10, 2006, from http://nces.ed.gov/pro-grams/digest/d03/tables/dt231.asp.

National Science Foundation. *Women, Minorities, and Persons with Disabilities in Sciences and Engineering: 2004.* Arlington, Va.: National Science Foundation, 2004.

Nosek, B. A., Banaji, M. R., and Greenwald, A. G. "Math = Male, Me = Female, Therefore Math [Not Equal to] Me." *Journal of Personality and Social Psychology*, 2002, *83*, 44–59.

Skrla, L., Reyes, P., and Scheurich, J. J. "Sexism, Silence, and Solutions: Women Superintendents Speak Up and Speak Out." *Educational Administration Quarterly*, 2000, *36*(1), 44–75.

"South African Women in Corporate Leadership Census, 2005." *Business Women's Association and Catalyst (USA).* Retrieved June 4, 2006, from http://www.catalystwomen.org/headlines/files/2005 percent20Census percent20of percent20South percent20African percent20Women percent20in percent20Corporate percent20Leadership.pdf.

Steele, J., James, J. B., and Barnett, R. C. "Learning in a Man's World: Examining the Perceptions of Undergraduate Women in Male-Dominated Academic Areas." *Psychology of Women Quarterly*, 2002, *26*, 46–50.

HILARY M. LIPS is professor of psychology, chair of the Psychology Department, and director of the Center for Gender Studies at Radford University.

6

This chapter provides background theory and practical steps for a possible selves approach to career development in adult education settings. It also identifies methods to foster development, enhance motivation, and manage setbacks.

Possible Selves and Career Transition: It's Who You Want to Be, Not What You Want to Do

Geoff Plimmer, Alison Schmidt

Desire for career change is the driver behind much adult study. Career change and going back to school as an adult are often stressful. For the individual, the experience typically begins with a state of dissatisfaction about who he or she is and who he or she is becoming. Dissatisfied adults who make major career changes generally become more satisfied than those who did not, suggesting that the associated struggle is usually worthwhile (Thomas, 1980).

Career transition often represents a radical break from earlier goals and plans. It may conflict with family obligations; it may involve trying out new roles and identities and revisiting past obstacles and fears (Schlossberg, 1984). Beneath the carefully written résumé, the reasons for seeking career change may be fraught with emotion, uncertainty, and the desire to be someone different. Possible selves theory, when applied to new approaches to career development and adult education, helps us understand how adults manage transition and move toward being the selves that they want to become.

This chapter outlines how possible selves theory is used in career development and how these uses might apply to adult learning. It draws on theory, practice, and, for illustration, vignettes from a study of mature students' experiences in a New Zealand polytechnic college (Schmidt, Mabbett, and Houston, 2005). It includes some personal conclusions taken from our

NEW DIRECTIONS FOR ADULT AND CONTINUING EDUCATION, no. 114, Summer 2007 © 2007 Wiley Periodicals, Inc.
Published online in Wiley InterScience (www.interscience.wiley.com) • DOI: 10.1002/ace.257

61

experience of using possible selves with clients and presents a five-step process to use with learners in developing effective possible selves. Each section ends with some practical career development techniques directed to adult educators.

Being a mature adult in career transition is different from being a younger person, though younger people are the chief concern of traditional learning and career theories (Taylor and Giannantonio, 1990). Mature adults interpret themselves and the world with more complexity than the young do (Hy and Loevinger, 1996), while also having a narrower and more specialized sense of self. Mature adults are less guided by social comparison and more guided by comparison with how they ideally want to be (Ouellete and others, 2005). Usually they are less malleable than younger people and may be experiencing an intense search for meaning (Zunker, 1990). Their sense of opportunity is often limited by obligations to others, as is Kim, a middle-aged woman who comments that "the biggest obstacle for me is my home commitments because I have four children and a family to run."

Adult learners may also have a sense of running out of time. William, a mature part-time student, is dispirited by what he calls his "protracted process" and is daunted by his realization that "I've got a six year process before I'm even qualified . . . at that stage I'll be 51 years old."

An adult who returns to study may be attempting to break out of a sense of limited opportunities and restricted roles. Back in an education setting, adults may find their deeply held assumptions, beliefs, and expectations threatened. Furthermore, mature adults can feel like impostors, culturally alien and isolated (Brookfield, 1999). Older people in career transition often see themselves as having fewer psychological resources; they may experience more stress and less progress and may perceive more barriers to change than younger people do (Heppner, Multon, and Johnston, 1994). These themes of stress, circumscription, search for meaning, complexity, and narrowing and consolidating the self are well traversed in the adult learning and adult careers literatures (Brown, Brooks, and Associates, 1996; Knowles, 1990; Zunker, 1990).

Issues of Self in Adult Learning Theory

Adult learning and career theories have often focused on the need for meaning and the use of past knowledge, but they have not always adequately considered changes in the self. In the adult education field, Knowles (1990) identified prior knowledge and experiences as central to the individual's learning experience. They provide a framework for understanding the purpose of learning, memory, and making sense of what is being learned. Adult learners have a strong need for self-direction and to apply their previous work-related experiences to their learning. More recently, Mezirow and Associates (2000) focus on the transformative nature of learning and the process through which past knowledge is altered. Learners' perspectives are transformed through a ten-step process that begins with a disorienting dilemma, followed by self-examination, and eventually leading to a new course of action, acquiring new knowledge and skills, trying on new roles, and integrating new learning into one's life (Taylor, 1998).

While Knowles (1990) and Mezirow and Associates (2000) concur on the significance of experience and the importance of personal goals, Mezirow's transformative learning approach has a greater focus on the future and the ways that past knowledge and the self are altered. Mezirow and Associates argue that there is a more profound change within the individual than the simple acquisition of new knowledge and qualifications. As people develop through learning, new goals and concepts of the future self emerge.

Just as adult education theories have shifted toward a more fundamental type of knowledge than declarative learning and a greater recognition of the whole person than traditional "talk-and-chalk" teaching approaches, so adult career development theory has taken a similar journey.

Issues of Self in Career Development Theory

Careers have changed over the past thirty years. Both jobs and the workforce are more diverse than previously, and new approaches and theories have been developed to explain careers and help people with career transition. Traditional approaches to career advice usually center on classifying people based on factors such as personality (Holland, 1985), stage of career (Super, 1992), and value-based anchors (Schein, 1993), followed by a matching to corresponding jobs. However, this focus on classification and matching misses much of the complexity and emotional intensity of what goes on in adult career change. Traditional approaches treat both people and careers as static rather than evolving. Consequently, career theories need to shift toward more holistic approaches that focus on adaptability rather than decision making and to recognize such features of adult career change as the need to consider both obligations to others and the search for meaning. In practice many career counselors have limited time and resources, so they need to cover a lot of ground quickly.

A focus on adaptability suits the modern world of work where jobs are more flexible than in the past. There is less security but more choice, and career change is more common. Adaptability goes beyond decision making to issues of performance and motivation. Emotion, whole life issues, individual context, and the development of self all need to be taken into account (Savickas, 1997). In practice, career changers need to become sufficiently self-aware to notice and respond to changes in both themselves and the world and to develop a repertoire of different identities, attitudes, and approaches and the skills to implement them (Savickas, 1997).

For people to develop adaptability, they need to be able to call on multiple identities, or selves, and to create new ones (Mirvis and Hall, 1994).

This enables them to develop long-term perspectives, manage relationships between the self and the outer world, and focus on the future (Savickas, 1997). They need to develop planful attitudes, self and environmental exploration skills, informed decision-making skills, and the capacity to recognize their own limitations in both abilities and self-concept.

Possible Selves and Career Change

Possible selves theory is a useful framework for people to manage changes in themselves. Each person has many possible selves that vary in importance, salience (how easy they are to recall and think about), and level of elaboration (how detailed, emotional, and vivid they are; King and Raspin, 2004). Possible selves reflect the images, senses, and thoughts people have about their future (Markus and Nurius, 1986). Possible selves are instrumental in personal and career change because they are changeable; they can liberate people from feeling trapped or restricted in their options. They provide a means of escape from current realities and constraints (Markus and Nurius, 1986), but they also provide a means of evaluating and giving meaning to events in the present. Possible selves can be well integrated with each other (my possible self that gets on well with people fits with my possible career self as a tour guide) or fractured (my career goal of being a facilitator conflicts with my feared possible self as an angry person). They tend to be interconnected through a web of life roles, beliefs, and identities that vary in the degree to which they are core, active, expected, and attached to the present.

As outlined in earlier chapters, possible selves can be positive (hopes) or negative (fears), and they can be rated as likely or unlikely. Hoped-for selves can include both ideal selves (whom you most want to be) and ought selves (whom you feel a duty or obligation to be) (Carver, Lawrence, and Scheier, 1999). This distinction between ideal and ought is conceptually similar to the distinction between intrinsic and extrinsic motivation in the self-determination literature and between learning and performance goals in the education literature (Elliott and Dweck, 1988; Ryan and Deci, 2000). Having intrinsic goals, such as those centered on community feelings, affiliation, health, and self-development, leads to higher performance, more effort and persistence, and reduced stress (Ryan and Deci, 2000). Emphasis on extrinsic factors or performance goals, such as money and status, leads to comparatively lower performance, resilience, and well-being.

While possible selves are related to both extrinsic and intrinsic motivation, a possible self approach in career work encourages more focus on intrinsic goals because of the integration with personal meanings. The approach therefore encourages more self-direction and determination and less social comparison and "keeping up with the Joneses." Using possible selves is also more holistic because the content of a possible self encompasses values, roles, lifestyles, self-beliefs, skills, and interests.

New Directions for Adult and Continuing Education • DOI: 10.1002/ace

Discussing possible selves with clients generally encourages a focus on who a person wants to be rather than what he or she wants to do. Possible selves serve as a bridge between self-concept and motivation (Ruvolo and Markus, 1992).

Possible selves aid career development through the operation of five mechanisms (Meara, Day, Chalk, and Phelps, 1995). The first is that possible selves are personalized and intensely individual. They reflect matters such as efficacy, values, and personalized meanings. They make the self central to career decision making. The second mechanism is that highly vivid images of success (or failure) often carry salient and elaborated self-concepts that are personally motivating, such as a student's vivid image of a graduation ceremony. The third characteristic is that they are laden with emotions such as happiness or insecurity, which can be personalized goals in themselves (Winell, 1987). These emotions can give meaning and can be energizing or demotivating. Emotions can become goals in the sense that people look forward to positive emotions and try to avoid negative ones.

The fourth mechanism is that possible selves contain the strategies and tactics to achieve career goals through schema that enable effective processing of information and knowledge and strategies to achieve them (Meara, Day, Chalk, and Phelps, 1995). Having a clear possible self often carries with it "mental software," called schema, to help a person become that self. Finally, as discussed by Lee and Oyserman (this volume), a balance of hopes and fears appears to be effectively motivating through the presence of avoidance goals (Meara, Day, Chalk, and Phelps, 1995). People find it easier to avoid a fear coming true if they have an alternative to hope for. And fears can be a good reality check.

How It Works: The Upbeat Stuff

Using possible selves in adult education encourages a positive and strengths-based approach to change and development. It helps people try on new roles and look to the future rather than the past. It can also provide a new and liberating frame of reference with which to interpret the world.

Change and Development. Changing career and returning to study changes people's identities and self-concepts. Part of this process is the development of new possible selves, which can be provisionally "created, tested, discarded and revised" to determine their fit (Ibarra, 1999, p. 765). During career transition, people use provisional selves that they develop through observation and testing to see whether they fit with their values, competencies, requirements, and style. People identify prototypes of what constitutes desirable performance and then match their identity to the prototypes. This creates a personalized repertoire of possible roles and selves. One way this happens is through studying others' styles and ways of working and then practicing emulating those styles to see whether they fit.

Focusing on a positive possible self can liberate people from less appealing current states. Positive possible selves often provide, or are associated with, feelings of mastery that are incentives for effective behaviors (Markus and Nurius, 1986). Consequently, development of positive futures provides more effective means of self-development than focusing on the present or past self-concept. In other words, focusing on "who I want to be" is often more valuable than focusing on "why am I like this?"

As positive possible selves become more elaborate and influential, they become useful new benchmarks for behavior. Past and present selves become less important or become negative points of comparison that are let go as perspectives change. Hill and Spokane (1995) found that career counseling increased the number and attractiveness of possible selves, while past selves declined in their appeal over several sessions.

Conversely, possible selves are sometimes based on past selves. Midlife career changes and return to studies are often about returning to a career plan vetoed by parents or interrupted for raising children. Often past possible selves are rediscovered and reused (King and Raspin, 2004). Bill, who had sold his hardware store to become a counselor, said this: "You know [the decision to study] brought a dimension into my life which I had given up once I'd become married and did all the roles that were necessary there, and I was really pleased to break out of those roles."

Through these processes of trying on prior and possible selves, focusing on the future, and letting go of or reinventing past selves, new values and choices for the future emerge, and fundamental assumptions about self and the world are challenged. A useful practical application of this is to map out past selves or life stages, including strengths and corresponding emotional states. This mapping can be done into the future as well as looking back to the past. A mapping exercise helps clients or students to develop meaningful future-related selves quickly, which they can then put into action.

Motivation and Performance. Possible selves explicitly aid current performance by providing schema for scanning and processing information in the present (Cross and Markus, 1994). They provide a framework in which a person can evaluate everyday occurrences. The schema attached to positive well-developed possible selves can determine what a person notices, remembers, and associates with the new information. Well-elaborated possible selves are likely to include some rehearsal and simulation, which also improves performance (Cross and Markus, 1994).

For career development, salient and vivid job-related possible selves provide schema that lead people to notice particular job advertisements, overcome the fear of résumé writing, and better plan job-seeking behaviors. In adult learning, possible selves create schema that help students notice and remember relevant course-related material (Fletcher, 2000). For example, a well-developed possible self as a successful sports coach is likely to include highly personalized images of helping people, being outdoors, and the like. Martin, a solo father of four boys, had a clear mental picture of a future in which he would have "all of these things to add to my CV, like the bachelor degree and all that together will add up. . . . I will pick up a $65k+ job and that's where I'm heading."

An individual with a well-developed concept of future self is more likely to attend to information linked to this schema and to connect relevant strands of information together, such as techniques, jobs, or opportunities to practice. In contrast, an individual without a relevant schema is less likely to attend to coaching-related information or effectively process or remember it. Having clear personal goals also enhances unconscious processes (Dijksterhuis, Aarts, and Smith, 2005). Research indicates that unconscious decision-making processes often lead to better decisions than conscious, rational thought processes. This is particularly true when decisions are important and complex and involve many trade-offs, as with career decisions (Dijksterhuis, Aarts, and Smith, 2005).

In career transition, people find added meaning and have more energy for difficult, stressful, or mundane tasks if they relate to a desired possible self. Consequently they can more easily overcome barriers. The successful coaching self may see a series of paths, including studying hard, making sacrifices, practicing in voluntary coaching roles, and eventually getting a paid, professional coaching position. For Doris, a mature therapeutic recreation student, a clear view of the end goal helped her to understand the relevance of the papers that she struggled writing. She says: "I can see the end result. . . . Like it's, all the papers sort of connect up to each other and I can see, oh yep, I know where that's going, and I know that at the end of this year I will know how to do certain things."

Possible selves link strongly to the benefits of goal setting because they help the individual to develop strategies to prioritize and allocate resources (Kanfer, 1994). When people make their possible selves more specific (that is, more vivid and concrete) and a consequence of their personal effort, this makes their goals more accessible and more achievable (Ruvolo and Markus, 1992). Narrowing the gap between "where you are now" and "where you want to go" through vivid imagery brings the desired end state closer and enhances motivation. In our practice, we have found that helping clients develop clear images of themselves in the future through quiet contemplation or writing exercises has a remarkable effect on persistence in areas like study and work.

When people develop clear pathways to help achieve their possible selves, they develop the will and find the means achieve them. They can do this because they are better able to plan, judge progress, and develop alternative courses of action (Oyserman and Markus, 1990). Discussing possible selves, their meanings, and pathways to achieve them are good exercises to assist adults in reaching their goals. Possible selves can provide energy for planning and action in areas where change is strongly desired but difficult such as initiating a job change.

How It Works: The Tough Stuff

Adult career transition, and learning and development, often involve hardship and setbacks. They are environments where self-delusion and other defense mechanisms occur, to the detriment of the learner. However, using possible selves can improve resiliency in the face of setbacks by helping to build implementation intentions, providing a richer repertoire of internal resources to draw on, and providing a framework for reality checks.

Dealing with Adversity and Setbacks. People fail to implement their goals for a number of reasons (Gollwitzer and Sheeran, 2006). They may get distracted and forget their goal at crucial times; situational cues may drive their behavior in alternative directions. In other words, people miss crucial opportunities to act in a way that will move them toward their goal. Personalized goals are more likely to be reached when there are clear plans for what, when, where, and how they can be implemented (Gollwitzer and Sheeran, 2006). In practice, for example, a person who has a possible self as a calm but assertive office professional may need very detailed micro goals to help overcome a likely fear of losing his or her temper at management meetings. A hoped-for self along these lines will more likely be realized if there are specific plans about, for example, what to do when certain individuals at management meetings make comments in a certain style. Such clear personalized micro goals are more likely to be developed and adhered to if they relate to a salient, important, and vivid possible self.

People vary in the complexity, number, and degree of interconnections of their self-concepts (Linville, 1985). Having many possible selves has advantages in managing well-being, partly because one possible self may turn out to be unrealizable. There is evidence also that people cope emotionally with life change more effectively if they have more complex future self-concepts (Niedenthal, Setterlund, and Wherry, 1992). The presence of complex, positive, and rich future self-concepts seems more important than the number and strength of negative selves in the present. Put another way, it is beliefs about the future that count in coping with life change rather than how bad things may seem in the present. In the Niedenthal, Setterlund, and Wherry study (1992), it was the existence of alternative possible selves that made the difference for people recovering from a crisis.

Desired possible selves provide buffers against setbacks because their links to self schema help people to develop alternative courses of action. In contrast, individuals without schema related to positive possible selves are more likely to be put off by setbacks because negative possible selves are more easily aroused (Cross and Markus, 1994), and they lack the capacity to process information and develop effective plans. The ability to develop courses of action within a framework of possible selves is illustrated by the case study of Kim, whose strong sense of direction helps when things go wrong. She says, "If it doesn't happen that way, or if I can't do it, or if there is a problem, then I sort of deviate slightly and move around it."

Dealing with Self-Deception. In career transition, people's expectations about the future are often insecure and unstable, and they may have unrealistic optimism and self-deception. Although self-deception and an optimistic bias do occur across past, present, and future self-concepts, future self-concepts seem particularly prone to distortion (Robinson and Ryff, 1999). This can be a good thing, because optimistic possible selves help focus energy, increase resilience, and can elicit better outcomes. But unrealistic optimism can also lead to poor decisions and misplaced effort. Optimistic self-deception is highest in early adulthood and seems to decline during the life course. Possible selves appear particularly prone to the effects of unrealistic optimism when people are low in information and motivational benefits are high. Unrealistic expectations of career opportunities after returning to study are an example of this.

Schemas act to protect the individual from negative information by screening out stimuli that are threatening and by favoring positive information (Greenwald, 1980). Depressed people lack this self-favoring bias and may seek out information that confirms negative schemas. Greenwald (1980) describes the self-protective mechanism as the "totalitarian ego," because it resembles the operation of totalitarian states. Opposing information is oppressed or discounted, and when new information is allowed in, it is interpreted in ways that serve to protect the self. Although this self-protective function is often beneficial, it can also be harmful and undermine the ability to manage risks. Heightening awareness of what parts of life or the self are not likely to change reduces self-deception (Robinson and Ryff, 1999).

Individuals' unrealistic and potentially harmful optimism can be reduced by helping them develop lists of what they think will and will not change across different parts of their life during career transition. Career exploration (research and information gathering) can also reduce optimistic self-deception. To avoid unrealistic pessimism, asking clients to write counterarguments against reasoning that likely feared selves will be realized can reduce anxiety and negative thinking. This abridged cognitive behavioral approach can be effective in dealing with adversity and setbacks and preventing the activation of feared selves (Plimmer, 2001).

Managing the Gap Among Actual, Ought, and Desired Selves. Identifying differences among actual, ought, and ideal selves helps clients understand their motivation and aspirations. Actual selves are who we are in the present tense. Ought selves are more future oriented and concern others' expectations (real or imagined) of who we ought to be. Ideal selves are also future oriented and concern who we would like to become, including wishes and aspirations for the self (Phillips and Silvia, 2005). Gaps among actual, ought, and ideal selves have effects on behavior and emotion. People appear to find that focusing on ideal rather than ought selves is more motivating, because ideal selves capture more personalized and intrinsic goals. Ideal selves are more salient at times when fears are considered to be less likely (Carver, Lawrence, and Scheier, 1999). There is some evidence that people who focus on who they want to be (ideal selves), more than what they think they ought to be, focus more on positive than negative information and seem more resistant to depressive thinking (Carver, Reynolds, and Scheier, 1994).

Self-awareness, a common goal of adult education and career transition, includes awareness of gaps between who one is and who one wants to be. Raising self-awareness can be upsetting as well as motivating (Phillips and Silvia, 2005), but providing positive, affirming information can reduce defensiveness, increase receptiveness to negative information, and facilitate its integration into the self-concepts (Schwinghammer, Stapel, and Blanton, 2006). This in turn means people can manage risks better, engage in planful foresight, and become increasingly adaptable. Adult educators are in a strong position to help people in this process (Rossiter, 2003).

Dealing with Fears. Possible selves approaches are effective in identifying and addressing the barriers that underlie career indecision (Parkin and Plimmer, 2004). When people discuss their fears, their self-efficacy beliefs, and their views of the world, this often provides a means to tackle the real issues. Feared possible selves, such as failure at law school, provide avoidance goals, which, when balanced with relevant hoped-for selves, increase motivation (Oyserman and Markus, 1990).

However, strongly feared selves can inhibit effective functioning if they are seen as inevitable and are not balanced by achievable hoped-for selves. Without this balance, feared selves can reduce performance by interfering with concentration and leading to distracted attention, reduced focus, and negative cognitions and affect (Csikszentmihalyi, 1988).

What This Means for Adult Education Practitioners

The practical advantages of developing possible selves in education and career transition are significant. What distinguishes possible selves from traditional goal-setting concepts are the emotion, values, and schema attached to them. Because possible selves include diverse aspects of human experience as well as specific career options, possible selves support career decision making and provide a much richer foundation to build a "bridge to the future" than traditional approaches (Martz, 2001, p. 131).

Acknowledging and working with possible selves is an empathic process in practice because it recognizes the whole person (Martz, 2001). The relationship building associated with possible selves-based education reduces defensiveness, builds self-awareness, and helps learners process information about work, study, and themselves more effectively. Working with possible selves reaches places in people that are missed by other approaches. By recognizing unique personal meanings, the possible selves approach can have an impact on cognition, affect, and expectancies (Cohen, Duberley, and Mallon, 2004).

New Directions for Adult and Continuing Education • DOI: 10.1002/ace

A Five-Step Approach

Adult educators can facilitate the development of positive new possible selves and their benefits to performance and motivation through a five-step process. This process involves developing understanding of possible selves, providing contextual and qualitative information about vocational options for learners, and helping learners to find the fit between their possible selves and occupational information. The fourth and fifth steps are elaborating desired possible selves and developing pathways to achieve them.

Step 1: Identify Possible Selves and Make Connections. The first step is to encourage discussion among learners about possible self factors such as values, skills, lifestyle preferences, career goals, hopes and fears, interests, and self beliefs. Building connections and identifying paradoxes across different possible selves enables individuals to develop richer self-understanding for decision making. Developing narratives of "where I've been" and "where I'm going" can add detail and an emotional dimension to possible self options. Narratives can be developed in text form or mind maps (looking forward). Future self software tools are effective in developing engagement with the process, addressing barriers, and ensuring comprehensive coverage of personalized self-representations quickly (Plimmer, 2001).

Step 2: Provide Information and Guidance. The second step is to provide contextual and qualitative information about careers that are relevant to the course or content being taught. Educators can provide more detailed and contextualized vocational knowledge than is available through formal career programs. By suggesting potential career opportunities and recognizing an individual's potential, educators can reduce the sense of lost possibilities or confirm existing original dreams and raise efficacy beliefs through encouragement (Rossiter, 2003).

Step 3: Find the Fit. The third step is helping students to compare the level of fit between their possible selves and career options. Helping learners to apply new learning to their developing self-concept—trying it on for size—allows possible selves to be elaborated. This builds on the foundations of Mezirow's perspective transformation (2000) by widening perspectives and paving the way for change. Enabling learners to observe a range of career identities, practice them, and relate them to their own envisaged selves fosters more internalized goal-related behavior than a more mechanistic, skill-based approach. Discussion and role plays enable learners to evaluate career possible selves and to ask, "Is this really who I want to be?" and "Does it feel right?"

Step 4: Focus on Strengths and Positive Futures. The goal of this stage is to develop clear and vivid representations of the self through techniques such as mental imagery (Fletcher, 2000), mental rehearsal, displaying symbols in private spaces such as diaries, and discussion with others.

New Directions for Adult and Continuing Education • DOI: 10.1002/ace

Step 5: Develop Positive Pathways. Although pathways often evolve naturally from possible selves, structured planning can be helpful. This can include setting goals for information seeking, goals to measure, or micro goals to overcome hard-to-change behaviors (Gollwitzer and Sheeran, 2006). In some ways, this pathway making is like getting ready for a road trip by filling the car with fuel and getting the maps ready. The exact route may not be known, but there is a general direction in mind, and the upcoming bridges, hills, valleys, and possibilities can be imagined.

Conclusion

Possible selves have particular strengths in adult education and career development because they cover the complexity of what matters as people age and because self is central to the process. Adults differ from younger people in terms of the increasing importance given to the search for meaning and the decreasing importance of comparison with others. "Who I want to be" is at the heart of what matters. The development of self is intensely personal, and the process changes people's perspectives in enduring ways. Because of this, the use of possible selves increases the likelihood of successful transition.

Possible selves serve as an umbrella concept under which many other educational and career development approaches can be used, which means that they are adaptable to the personal styles of good educators who wish to help learners achieve their personal goals. They offer a strengths-based approach that emphasizes goals rather than problems. At the same time, their relevance to barriers takes into account the stress and anxiety common in the real-life experience of career change and adult learning.

References

Brookfield, S. D. "What Is College Really Like for Adult Students?" *About Campus*, 1999, *3*(6), 10–15.

Brown, D., Brooks, L., and Associates. *Career Choice and Development.* (3rd ed.) San Francisco: Jossey-Bass, 1996.

Carver, C. S., Lawrence, J. W., and Scheier, M. F. "Self-Discrepancies and Affect: Incorporating the Role of Feared Selves." *Personality and Social Psychology Bulletin*, 1999, *25*(7), 783–792.

Carver, C. S., Reynolds, S. L., and Scheier, M. F. "The Possible Selves of Optimists and Pessimists." *Journal of Research in Personality*, 1994, *28*(2), 133–141.

Cohen, L., Duberley, J., and Mallon, M. "Social Constructionism in the Study of Career: Accessing the Parts That Other Approaches Cannot Reach." *Journal of Vocational Behavior*, 2004, *64*, 407–422.

Cross, S., and Markus, H. R. "Self-Schemas, Possible Selves, and Competent Performance." *Journal of Educational Psychology*, 1994, *86*, 423–438.

Csikszentmihalyi, M. "The Flow Experience and Its Significance for Human Psychology." In M. Csikszentmihalyi and I. S. Csikszentmihalyi (eds.), *Optimal Experience: Psychological Studies of Flow in Consciousness.* Cambridge: Cambridge University Press, 1988.

Dijksterhuis, A., Aarts, H., and Smith, P. K. "The Power of the Subliminal: Perception and Possible Applications." In R. Hassin, J. Uleman, and J. A. Bargh (eds.), *The New Unconscious*. New York: Oxford University Press, 2005.

Elliott, E. S., and Dweck, C. S. "Goals: An Approach to Motivation and Achievement." *Journal of Personality and Social Psychology*, 1988, *54*(1), 5–12.

Fletcher, S. "A Role for Imagery in Mentoring." *Career Development International* 2000, *5*, 2000, 235–243.

Gollwitzer, P. M., and Sheeran, P. "Implementation Intentions and Goal Achievement: A Meta-Analysis of Effects and Processes." *Advances of Experimental Social Psychology*, 2006, *38*, 69–119.

Greenwald, A. G. "The Totalitarian Ego: Fabrication and Revision of Personal History." *American Psychologist*, 1980, *35*, 603–618.

Heppner, M. J., Multon, K. D., and Johnston, J. A. "Assessing Psychological Resources During Career Change: Development of the Career Transitions Inventory." *Journal of Vocational Behavior*, 1994, *44*(4), 55–74.

Hill, A. L., and Spokane, A. R. "Career Counseling and Possible Selves: A Case Study." *Career Development Quarterly*, 1995, *43*, 221–232.

Holland, J. L. *Making Vocational Choices: A Theory of Careers.* Upper Saddle River, N.J.: Prentice Hall, 1985.

Hy, L. X., and Loevinger, J. *Measuring Ego Development.* (2nd ed.) Mahwah, N.J.: Erlbaum, 1996.

Ibarra, H. "Provisional Selves: Experimenting with Image and Identity in Professional Adaptation." *Administrative Science Quarterly*, 1999, *44*, 764–791.

Kanfer, R. "Work Motivation: New Directions in Theory and Research." In C. L. Cooper and I. T. Robertson (eds.), *Key Reviews in Managerial Psychology: Concepts and Research for Practice.* Hoboken, N.J.: Wiley, 1994.

King, L. A., and Raspin, C. "Lost and Found Possible Selves, Subjective Well-Being, and Ego Development in Divorced Women." *Journal of Personality and Social Psychology*, 2004, *72*, 603–732.

Knowles, M. *The Adult Learner: A Neglected Species.* Houston: Gulf Publishing, 1990.

Linville, P. W. "Self Complexity and Affective Extremity: Don't Put All Your Eggs in One Basket." *Social Cognition*, 1985, *3*, 94–120.

Markus, H., and Nurius, P. "Possible Selves." *American Psychologist,* 1986, *41*, 954–969.

Martz, E. "Expressing Counselor Empathy Through the Use of Possible Selves." *Journal of Employment Counseling*, 2001, *38*(3), 128–133.

Meara, N. M., Day, J. D., Chalk, L. M., and Phelps, R. E. "Possible Selves: Applications for Career Counseling." *Journal of Career Assessment*, 1995, *3*, 259–277.

Mezirow, J. E., and Associates. *Learning as Transformation: Critical Perspectives on a Theory in Progress.* San Francisco: Jossey-Bass, 2000.

Mirvis, P. H., and Hall, D. T. "Psychological Success and the Boundaryless Career." *Journal of Organizational Behaviour*, 1994, *15*, 365–380.

Niedenthal, P. M., Setterlund, M. B., and Wherry, M. B. "Possible Self-Complexity and Affective Reactions to Goal-Relevant Evaluation." *Journal of Personality and Social Psychology*, 1992, *63*(1), 5–16.

Ouellete, J. A., and others. "Using Images to Increase Exercise Behavior: Prototypes Versus Possible Selves." *Personality and Social Psychology Bulletin*, 2005, *5*, 610–620.

Oyserman, D., and Markus, H. "Possible Selves in Balance: Implications for Delinquency." *Journal of Social Issues*, 1990, *46*, 141–157.

Parkin, F., and Plimmer, G. "Managing the Presence of Personal Issues in Career Counselling: Using Transactional Analysis with Possible Selves." *Australian Journal of Career Development*, 2004, *13*(1), 7–14.

Phillips, A. G., and Silvia, P. J. "Self-Awareness and the Emotional Consequences of Self-Discrepancies." *Personality and Social Psychology Bulletin*, 2005, *31*, 703–713.

Plimmer, G. "Development and Evaluation of a Career Development Intervention Using Modern Theories of the Self." Unpublished doctoral dissertation, Victoria University of Wellington, 2001.

Robinson, M. D., and Ryff, C. D. "The Role of Self-Deception in Perceptions of Past, Present, and Future Happiness." *Personality and Social Psychology Bulletin,* 1999, *25,* 595–606.

Rossiter, M. "Constructing the Possible: A Study of Educational Relationships and Possible Selves." Paper presented at the Forty-Fourth Annual Adult Education Research Conference, San Francisco, 2003.

Ruvolo, A. P., and Markus, H. R. "Possible Selves and Performance: The Power of Self-Relevant Imagery." *Social Cognition,* 1992, *10,* 95–124.

Ryan, R. M., and Deci, E. L. "Self-Determination Theory and the Facilitation of Intrinsic Motivation, Social Development, and Well-Being." *American Psychologist,* 2000, *55,* 68–78.

Savickas, M. L. "Career Adaptability: An Integrative Construct for Life Span, Life Space Theory." *Career Development Quarterly,* 1997, *45,* 246–259.

Schein, E. H. *Career Anchors: Discovering Your Real Values.* San Francisco: Jossey-Bass/Pfeiffer, 1993.

Schlossberg, N. K. *Counseling Adults in Transition: Linking Practice with Theory.* New York: Springer, 1984.

Schmidt, A., Mabbett, T., and Houston, D. "Retention and Success in Tertiary Education: 'It's a Belonging Thing.'" Paper presented at the New Zealand Association of Bridging Educators Conference, Auckland, 2005.

Schwinghammer, S. A., Stapel, D. A., and Blanton, H. "Different Selves Have Different Effects: Self-Activation and Defensive Social Comparison." *Personality and Social Psychology Bulletin,* 2006, *32*(1), 27–39.

Super, D. E. "Toward a Comprehensive Theory of Career Development." In D. H. Montross and C. J. Shinkman (eds.), *Career Development: Theory and Practice.* Springfield, Ill.: Charles C. Thomas, 1992.

Taylor, E. W. *The Theory and Practice of Transformative Learning: A Critical Review.* Columbus, Ohio: ERIC Clearinghouse on Adult, Career, and Vocational Education, 1998. (ED 423 422)

Taylor, M. S., and Giannantonio, C. M. "Vocational Guidance." *International Review of Industrial and Organisational Psychology,* 1990, *5,* 281–323.

Thomas, L. E. "A Typology of Mid Life Career Changers." *Journal of Vocational Behaviour,* 1980, *16,* 173–182.

Winell, M. "Personal Goals: The Key to Self-Direction in Adulthood." In M. E. Ford and D. H. Ford (eds.), *Humans as Self-Constructing Living Systems: Putting the Framework to Work.* Mahwah, N.J.: Erlbaum, 1987.

Zunker, V. G. *Career Counselling: Applied Concepts of Life Planning.* Pacific Grove, Calif.: Brooks/Cole, 1990.

GEOFF PLIMMER *is director of FutureSelves Ltd. and lectures on training and development topics at the Management School at Victoria University of Wellington, New Zealand.*

ALISON SCHMIDT *is an adviser to the New Zealand Qualifications Authority.*

7

This chapter explores how incorporating the possible selves construct within a supportive and challenging mentoring relationship can assist in personal and professional growth.

Mentoring Adult Learners: Realizing Possible Selves

Sarah Fletcher

In our lives, forces are at work that describe and define us in ways that undermine our ability to envision, imagine, and realize future possibilities in ourselves. We are labeled and categorized from birth by ethnic group, size, intelligence, socioeconomic status, and more. Such labels can be empowering and enable us to gain access to resources that assist our development. Or they can be straitjackets that condemn us to remain in a certain subset of the population, never actualizing our potential as learners. We need to be aware of our capacity to "be" beyond constraining labels and take responsibility for who we are and who we want to become. How do we improve our lot if we do not or cannot take responsibility for our own development? Is it enough to accept that we must work within an imposed categorization, especially if we are unlucky enough to be born into a disadvantaged group?

The possible selves construct has been largely unexplored as a basis for transformation. Previous chapters have already explained how the possible selves construct has evolved through the work of Hazel Markus and others. My own encounter came through reading a study by Leondari, Syngollitou, and Kiosseoglou (1998) in 2000. As a self-directed adult learner, I had been mentored and had self-mentored my own professional and personal development for many years in teacher education. I used the possible selves construct to assist me in defining who I wanted to become, ensuring I was grounded in the possible as well as the enticingly desirable. Working from my own experience in being mentored to overcome illness, I began to embed Markus's ideas

in professional development opportunities that I offered others. This chapter offers a perspective on using the possible selves construct in mentoring that will be useful to professional developers in many contexts.

The realization of possible selves occurs in a social dialogic context. Mentoring relationships constitute one such context that can help those involved to realize their potential. It is my premise that incorporating the possible selves construct originated by Markus and Nurius (1986) within a collaboratively supportive and challenging mentoring relationship can assist in personal growth and the improvement of practice. Integrating self-study action research into mentoring enables mentor and mentee to undertake sustained and systematic inquiry into their development. This in turn enables them to understand the changes that they have initiated and offers insights regarding the creation of more effective forms of human development programs.

Markus and Ruvolo (1989) suggest that "most goals occasion the construction of a possible self in which one is different from a now self and in which one realises the goal" (p. 212). These possible selves are "future orientated components of the self-system [which] represent individuals' ideas of what they might become" (p. 212). Markus and Ruvolo further suggest that constructing and envisioning a possible self having attained a goal may serve to connect the goal to specific actions that lead to its achievement. In an earlier article about incorporating a possible selves construct in mentoring (Fletcher, 2000b), I ventured the opinion that possible selves can, or so it seems, be consciously conjured up in the pursuit of desired goals that can be positively or negatively construed. Possible selves are thought to influence the motivation process in two ways: on the one hand, for providing a clear goal to strive for if they are positive and to avoid if they are negative and, on the other hand, by energizing an individual to pursue the actions necessary for attaining a possible self.

I still value the possible self-construct for professional enhancement when embedded in mentoring.

I begin this chapter with a discussion of mentoring as a transformational relationship for continuing personal and professional renewal, including structuring a supporting culture within which to mentor adult learners. I then explore the following aspects of mentoring in relation to enabling possible selves:

- Using imagery, metaphor, and visualization to define, refine, and enact possible selves
- Using digital technology to explore the present actual self as a basis for change
- Integrating action research within mentoring to support emerging possible selves
- Using collaborative inquiry as a means to benefit the mentor and the mentee

New Directions for Adult and Continuing Education • DOI: 10.1002/ace

The chapter ends with a discussion of the pros and cons of the use of possible selves in mentoring.

Mentoring as a Transformational Relationship

Mentoring and coaching have often been given poor press in relation to school-based practice in recent years. Although perceived as an important means to transformation, especially for the downtrodden, they have been ill defined and often ill implemented as a cheap solution to initial staff training in education. Because mentoring and coaching tend to be tacked on to other activities, the enormous creative potential for life-changing actualization has too often been lost. The mentor is robbed of necessary development opportunities, and the mentee is left largely to his or her own devices despite mentoring or coaching interventions. It does not have to be that way. Mentoring, including the crucial component of coaching, can be transformational for the individual, for the organization in which he or she works, and in family and friendship circles. In my experience as a mentor working with adult learners, professional sports coaches, nurses, and nurse educators, as well as with mentors in the police force, it is clear that the possible selves construct can enable transformation.

Mullen and Lick (1999) have shown that mentoring can be a synergistic process where collaborative efforts toward improvement can assist in bringing about life-enhancing change. In focusing on school-based mentoring, I (2000a) talked about mentoring as continuing personal and professional change (CPPD), and my recent research has explored mentoring within andragogy (Knowles, 1980), which complements pedagogy. Chipping and Morse (2006) recount how mutual research mentoring has enabled them to radically alter their perception of mentoring as top-down imposition and nonenabling experience to one of mutual revitalizing benefit. They comment: "One of our greatest discoveries was that mentoring is a two-way learning process. In the past we had always wrongly assumed that the people mentoring us were the authority and had completed all the learning they needed. We had not considered that the whole mentoring process was a learning tool for the mentor too. The experience of research mentoring created a new and rejuvenated enthusiasm for [our] professional development and for the profession of teaching itself" (p. 3).

If it is to stand a chance of bringing about constructive and life-enhancing transformation, mentoring cannot thrive in an organizational vacuum. It must be embedded as a central premise on which the organization is founded and runs on a daily basis. This applies equally well to mentoring in teacher and nurse education, mentoring for the police, and for the armed forces. Mentoring must be accorded sufficient creative space, time, and status. Mentors need support from other mentors for sustaining their professional development.

The pump-priming system (one or two intensive mentor training days) is not sufficient in itself to engender a culture in which employees can have ongoing meaningful professional development opportunities. Not all employees will make good mentors, but all mentors must be sufficiently skilled and experienced in their profession that they are respected by others. This is not to say that mentors must necessarily be older than their mentees, but they must be in a position to open up opportunities for mentees and to be able to focus on mentoring without fear about their own capacity to do their work. Most of all they must want to be mentors and be open to learning and not try to provide all the answers.

Defining, Refining, and Enacting Possible Selves Through Mentoring

As a mentoring relationship begins to develop, there should be increasing trust between both parties. Mentoring must provide a safe space where possible selves can be defined and refined and where the sometimes painful, and always challenging, process of deep personal and professional transformation can occur. How does a mentor begin the process of assisting another person to explain whom they wish to become as the basis for enabling development? What kinds of questions might they ask to stimulate and sustain reflective practice? What are the ethical dimensions of disclosure in relation to using the possible selves construct as a central premise in a collaborative mentoring relationship? How might a mentor assist a mentee to recognize whom he or she is as a basis for whom he or she might wish to become? How might a mentor nurture more generative mentoring?

Defining and Visualizing Possible Selves Through Mentoring. There needs to be some systematic and supportive way of assisting mentees to accept that they may well need to learn and develop new skills, values, and understandings. Simply telling someone that they need to learn x, y, and z results in the kind of mentoring relationship that Chipping and Morse (2006) so roundly reject in their writing. Rachele Morse highlights dangers in dictatorial mentoring in a Web-based snapshot using a cartoon-type image subtitled, "You WILL learn from me!" Donna Chipping (2005) sees mentoring as mutual enrichment.

Within a work-based context, aspects of inducting a mentee into developing specified skills, values, and understandings exist. Mentoring enables transition, and it has been variously described as a means of guiding less experienced colleagues through difficult transitions in their careers, a means of bolstering their professional and their personal growth, and a two-way opportunity for the growth of educational knowledge. It is not synonymous with cloning, because it means developing individuals' strengths to maximize their professional and personal potential. Asking questions is not enough as modeling.

How does a mentor assist a mentee to develop specific skills through their relationship? As a starting point, the mentor needs to assist the mentee in auditing who he or she is and needs to become. The ensuing process of transition is far more likely to succeed when mentees feel they are at the helm, with expert guidance on hand when needed. If they are to be self-reliant once the mentoring relationship ends, mentees must know that they are the driving force in bringing about positive change.

What strategies can mentors employ to assist mentees to audit who they are? Asking, "What skills do you bring to this job?" may elicit aspects of an initial audit. But often, in my experience, mentees resist such direct questioning at first for fear of revealing weaknesses, or they are so self-deprecating that the mentor discovers all too late that a mentee already has a battery of relevant skills and understandings on which to draw. Initial probing about preexisting skills usually needs to be more subtle. Some mentees are happy to select descriptors from a bank of alternatives to represent their selves as they are now. Others are happy to sketch who they are in their current roles. Choosing a photographic image is another way of providing a focal point for a discussion between mentor and mentee to communicate a baseline audit from which to grow a self.

When I worked alongside Donna Chipping, her chosen image of herself as a novice researcher helped me to understand her feelings about taking on master's-level studies (Chipping, 2005). I could see she was excited as well as scared and that my mentoring needed to assist her in developing confidence in her own abilities. In working with Rachele Morse, I was aware from her choice of image that she did not want or need me to tell her what to do. Having established some insights into my mentees' now selves as they came into their new roles as teacher researchers, I could work with them to envision possible selves. In so doing, I could target coaching them in specific skills—for example, critical engagement with literature—and I could learn from them too. From Morse (2005), I learned new perspectives on creativity as she showed me her image about a new self, a mind exploding with ideas. She talked about freeing the imagination. I had not thought about creativity within the mind bursting to be released but rather more about inputting wavelengths to draw it out. Chipping, meanwhile, was helping me to understand new ways to depict multiplicity of self, which had been a focus of my self-study research for several years (Fletcher, 2003).

In 2000, when I wrote about a role for imagery in mentoring, I was working with a group of novice teachers. I experimented with assisting them to use relaxation and visualization techniques to define present selves and explore positive possible selves they wished to be. The preservice teachers who took part in using imagery were coming to the end of a thirty-six-week course leading to the award of the postgraduate certificate in education (PGCE). As a means to probe their own values and understandings about teaching, I showed the group a large-format photograph of a child in a schoolroom and asked them to vocalize how the image made them feel and what they wanted to do when they saw the girl.

Another exercise I tried was to ask them to remember or conjure up an interview situation where tricky questions were being asked and to face their reactions at feeling ill-at-ease. This strategy was designed as a kind of desensitization to lessen their fear at being put at a disadvantage at an interview-an experience that is a source of worry for novice teachers. By putting them at ease in a safe space and teaching them simple relaxation techniques to help them cope with interview nerves, I wanted to help them prepare for being the best possible selves they could be when on an interview. By imagining they were looking at the interviewer's face in a controlled situation, they could rehearse managing the nervousness that might prevent them (and in some cases had prevented them) from giving their best. I asked them to imagine themselves giving the answer that they would have wanted to give and to monitor their reactions as they did so. The exercises were well received by the group, and they said they found them very useful. In addition (and this was unexpected), I realized I was relating in a much more personal and individual way with each member of the group than I had done for the previous year. This enabled me to become the PGCE tutor that I wanted to be, enabling their successes.

As a mentor, I had begun to explore a potential for using visualization in my own practice in order to improve it. I realized visualization could assist mentoring in the following ways:

• By reinforcing positive self-images in the mentee's new role
• By sensitizing the mentee to new experiences in the new role
• By sharing the experiences of a mentor as a focus for adults learning
• By forming positive possible selves for the mentor and mentee to actualize
• By priming the self-system to prepare to take on new skills and roles

Using Visualization and Metaphor to Refine Possible Selves Through Mentoring. The techniques of visualization and metaphor can be used to help refine possible selves. Visualization techniques can be self-taught from the plethora of books, videos, and online resources that the Internet offers. Self-access courses are available, as are instructor-led programs (in my case, I learned to visualize in a pain clinic). Sean Whiteley (2001) offers simple generic techniques and explains the holistic experience of visualization. He identifies steps to visualization and presents ideas that a mentor might work on with a mentee, using images as a basis for dialogue.

Metaphor can provide an insight into the nature of the possible self that a mentee wishes to enact, but using metaphor and imagery can present problems, especially in cross cultural mentoring. Taking Reddy's conduit metaphor (1979), in which language functions like a conduit transferring thoughts from one person to another, Nomura (1993) demonstrates that the metaphor cannot be directly translated into Japanese as a word—it is a more fluid concept than in English. This means that the thoughts of one person would and could not be transmitted in their original form to another person without leakage of some of the original idea. Nevertheless, exploring metaphor provides a potentially rich vein to explore in mentoring.

Using Digital Technology to Enact Possible Selves Through Mentoring. Having identified with your mentee the parameters of the possible self he or she wishes to work toward as a means of improving his or her practice, mentoring as collaborative inquiry can begin in earnest. Where the professional context permits, it can be useful to combine visualization for internalized awareness with digital still and video technology as a means to validate claims to improving practice. Videoing as part of auditing the now-self activity provides a helpful archive for comparison with enacted possible selves. A mentor can act as a data collector as a mentee learns to change how he or she participates in his or her environment, acting as a "critical friend" by challenging assumptions.

Chipping and Morse have used Web-based technology to create an archive of their development as research mentors. Using photographs, video, and textual representation, they communicate how they evolved from unwilling participants in mentoring in initial teacher training to becoming so enthralled with research mentoring that they have taught their students the techniques. (For their contribution to educational knowledge, arrived at through systematic research, see Chipping, 2005).

Donna Chipping has used the KEEP template from the Carnegie Foundation. The aim of the KEEP Toolkit is to explore and create distinct forms and models that help faculty and educational institutions document, share, and reflect on some of the critical aspects of their efforts in transforming teaching and student learning. The toolkit is a set of web-based tools that help teachers create compact and engaging knowledge representations on the Web. With the KEEP Toolkit, teachers can transform materials into new formats and share their ideas with other teachers. The lessons in the toolkit are simple to use and can incorporate multimedia forms of representation. This medium contributes to the generative impact of mentoring, which sets in motion a chain of professional and personal development that is perceived as so life enhancing that one generation of mentors then inducts a further generation of mentors. Using Web-based technology such as the KEEP template, it becomes possible to create a resource bank of case studies from which mentors can draw ideas when initiating new mentoring relationships.

Rachele Morse has embedded video clips about the impact of mentoring on supporting her learning. Probing questions that might be off-putting at the start of a mentoring relationship (for example, "Who are you and who do you want to become in your professional life?") can become embedded in examining the depictions of possible selves represented by others. In my mentoring, I regularly draw on others' KEEP Toolkit snapshots.

Integrating Mentoring and Action Research for Enabling Possible Selves

By focusing on the visualization of a positive, possible self, I have incorporated some of the research by Markus and Ruvolo (1989) in my study. I believe this is the key to undertaking a living study of one's professional development, where the possible self is the goal emerging in practice and attained through action research. This is a communal model of self-study, facilitated through co-research mentoring.

In addition, I (Fletcher, 2006) integrate action research (McNiff and Whitehead, 2006) in mentoring. Such integration permits professional development for the mentor and the mentee as they examine their own present actual selves and explore their own future possible selves. Whitehead's model of self-study action research is an invaluable approach to assisting with practitioners' professional development (McNiff and Whitehead, 2006; see also McNiff and Whitehead, n.d., for a useful guide to action research).

A professional dialogue emerges as the mentoring relationship focuses on each question and aspect of the cycle depicted in Figure 7.1. The figure represents a much simplified schematic overview of what can occur and should not be slavishly followed as a step-by-step procedure. Mentoring is as much about listening and working in a creative way as a systematic and preplanned one. It is about listening and creating supportive scaffolds as well as probing.

Figure 7.1 is a representation of the focal points that a collaborating mentor and mentee using the possible selves construct might consider. The question cycle starts with, "What are my own core professional values?"

Figure 7.1. A Model of Mentoring Integrated with Action Research That Focuses on Elicitation and Actualization of Possible Selves to Improve Professional Practice

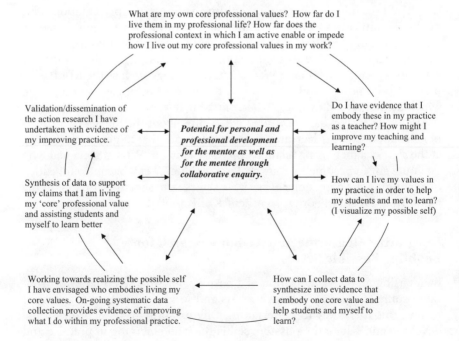

I recommend sustained and systematic reflection using questions of this kind to bring about awareness as a basis for action research. My approach to action research rests on exploring professional values, skills, and understandings that already exist as a basis for improving professional practice. Exploring emotions is just as important as exploring rationalized self-data. This approach is similar to Mezirow's notion (1991) about the importance of reflection on what has occurred as a basis for transformative learning. If the basis of constructing new possible selves rests on a critical engagement through reflection with previous and existing selves, there is a platform for the construction of possible selves to be realized. I suggest that the mentor and mentee use one another as professional sounding boards as they explore the questions that I have suggested. The mentor can usefully assist in collecting, collating, and analyzing self-data as the mentee undertakes self study.

The mentor has a crucial role to play in assisting mentees to understand who they are and who they have been as they construct new selves that are both positive and attainable. There is fertile ground for much mutual learning here. As the mentors assist mentees, they can reflect on their own practice as a basis for improvement. The mentor's practice, as well as the mentee's, is open to review in the model of mentoring-action research and possible self construction.

The suggestions for the use of photographic still and video images suggested by Mitchell and Weber (1999) are invaluable in the elicitation of adult learning here. They draw on the work of Max van Manen (1990) and include an extract of van Manen's approach to investigating lived experience that involves uncovering memory through the use of a particular example or experience. The incident or example is first described from an internal perspective and then in terms of the experience of living through it.

The Possible Selves Construct in Mentoring: Pros and Cons

There are no quick fixes in assisting adult learners to restructure and reinvent their own professional identities. Mentoring in a sensitive and empathetic way can assist both mentor and mentee to explore, define, and refine a possible self. A new possible self can become a goal toward which to work within a systematic and supportive program of critical friendship. But mentoring cannot exist in a culture that spawns subservience and stifles freedom. Exploring possible selves is risky. There is overt danger where mentoring incorporates assessment. Can the mentee afford to drop guard and confide in the mentor, who will decide if he or she remains in the organization? Can the mentee risk exposing ideas to criticism before they are more fully considered?

One of the more successful techniques that I employed when working with the possible selves construct with novice teachers was to ask them to videotape their own teaching (or ask their mentor to do so) and then select three brief episodes that showed them as the teacher they wanted to be.

New Directions for Adult and Continuing Education • DOI: 10.1002/ace

They would then show their mentor the sections and explain how and why they felt they were embodying the possible self they wanted to become as a teacher. This was supplemented by an exercise in which novice teachers showed three chosen episodes to one another and then peer-mentored each other highlighting what good practice they saw. This provided a positive and motivating experience that seemed to reassure the novices. Where criticism was offered it was from a peer and less daunting than from someone perceived as an expert.

Conclusion

Incorporating possible selves into mentoring, which in turn is integrated into self-study action research, can be a powerful change force in adult education. It can empower adult learners to take responsibility for their professional development and create a scaffold rather than a straitjacket within which they can continue to develop. Adult learners realize that they bear responsibility for communicating the possible self they want to work toward. A mentor cannot create a possible self for a mentee without endangering the synergy of the mentoring relationship. A mentor needs to have patience and capacity to listen without jumping to premature conclusions. He or she needs to be able to reflect back ideas in an empathetic way, gently steering a mentee to understand if the projected possible self is outside the realms of possibility. Taking an audit to provide a baseline for further targeted professional development is essential to the mentoring process. The mentor must be open to change too. He or she must embrace the idea of being an adult learner who does not and cannot provide all of the answers.

Why do I avidly promote inclusion of the possible selves construct in my practice? I have personal experience of its life-changing potential. From the perspective of being a disabled individual who was facing retirement in my thirties, I can endorse claims of life enhancement. This extract from my personal journal of 1987 shows how I used the possible selves construct to envision what I could become:

> The moment I knew I was healing myself was one of the funniest I shall ever remember. Encased in plaster from just below my armpits to my knee there was "I" seeing myself running, dancing and playing with friends on a beach! Momentary projection. Pain, searing pain machete-ing through my visualization—don't panic! Hold, hold on to the certainty that you will not falter in experiencing health. Draw from your being this agony and gently, gently ease it into vision. Initially, so all pervasive, this pain becomes a ball. Initially so immobile, it begins to move—it becomes a BALL! It bounces—I can play—and there I am—a child with a ball—a ball of pain. What do I do with this ball? Easy! I colour this ball, add stripes and fair-isle patterns like knitwear .... This ball of pain—this pain ball—no longer daunts me! I have a choice—an ultimate choice—to let it return to all-embracing agony—or to retain the ball, I bounce

this ridiculous sphere round the walls of my imagination—it loses its horror and I am reborn as a new "self," a self that knows health is closer [Fletcher, 2000b].

In my experience, the construct of possible selves is best embedded in a supportive and challenging collaborative mentoring experience. The benefits from such a relationship are potentially mutual for both the mentor and the mentee, but such a relationship can thrive only where there is a culture that sees risk taking and occasional failure as part of a rich learning process rather than as a threat to the organization involved. Imagery, metaphor, and visualization can assist in helping to define and refine not only a new self that a mentee strives for but also the creative process that enables its realization. Where mentoring provides a scaffolding experience that is structured but not constraining and where it is integrated with a systematic underpinning of self-study action research, the emergence of possible selves is a deep, rich learning experience for all involved. Digital technology offers a dynamic and exciting means to share learning experiences.

References

Chipping, D. "Work Based Mentoring and Action Research." 2005. Retrieved from http://www.cfkeep.org/html/snapshot.php?id=51952540922866.

Chipping, D., and Morse, R. *Using a Supportive Mentoring Relationship to Aid Independent Action Research.* London: DfES and the National Teacher Research Panel, 2006.

Fletcher, S. J. *Mentoring: A Handbook of Good Practice.* London: Routledge-Falmer, 2000a.

Fletcher, S. J. "A Role for Imagery in Mentoring." *Career Development International,* 2000b, 5(4/5), 235–243.

Fletcher, S. J. "Improving Mentoring with Action Research and Digital Video Technology." *Links Bulletin,* 2002, 25, 25–26.

Fletcher, S. J. "How Do I, a Professional Educator, Nurture Courage to Be?" Unpublished doctoral dissertation, University of Bath, 2003.

Fletcher, S. J. "Technology-Enabled Action Research in Mentoring Teacher Researchers." *Reflecting Education Journal,* 2006, 2(1), 50–71.

Knowledge Media Lab. *KEEP Toolkit.* Stanford, Calif.: Carnegie Foundation for the Advancement of Teaching. Retrieved from http://www.cfkeep.org/static/about/about.html.

Knowles, M. S. *The Modern Practice of Adult Education: From Pedagogy to Andragogy.* Cambridge, Mass.: Adult Education Company, 1980.

Leondari, A., Syngollitou, E., and Kiosseoglou, G. "Academic Achievement, Motivation and Future Selves." *Educational Studies,* 1998, 24(2), 53–163.

Markus, H., and Nurius, P. "Possible Selves." *American Psychologist,* 1986, 41, 954–969.

Markus, H., and Ruvolo, A. "Possible Selves: Personalized Representations of Goals." In L. Pervin (ed.), *Goal Concepts in Personality and Social Psychology.* Mahwah, N.J.: Erlbaum, 1989.

McNiff, J., and Whitehead, J. *All You Need to Know About Action Research.* Thousand Oaks, Calif.: Sage, 2006.

McNiff, J., and Whitehead, J. "Action Research with Jean McNiff." 2006. Retrieved on April 24, 2007 from http://www.jeanmcniff.com.

Mezirow, J. *Transformative Dimensions of Adult Learning.* San Francisco: Jossey-Bass, 1991.

Mitchell, C. and Weber, S. *Reinventing Ourselves as Teachers: Beyond Nostalgia.* London: Falmer Press, 1999.

Morse, R. "How Big Is Your Imagination?" (2005). Retrieved from http://www.cfkeep.org/html/snapshot.php?id=40142960511281.

Mullen, C., and Lick, D. *New Directions in Mentoring: Creating a Culture of Synergy.* London: Falmer Press, 1999.

Nomura, M. "Language as Fluid: A Description of the Conduit Metaphor in Japanese." *Kansas Working Papers in Linguistics,* 1993, *18,* 75–90.

Ortony, A., ed. *Metaphor and Thought.* Cambridge: Cambridge University Press, 1979.

Reddy, M. J. *The Conduit Metaphor: Metaphor and Thought.* Cambridge: Cambridge University Press, 1979.

van Manen, M. *Researching Lived Experience: Human Science for an Action Sensitive Pedagogy.* Albany, N.Y.: State University of New York Press, 1990.

Whiteley, S. "Using Visualization for Learning." Retrieved April 24, 2007 from http://www.trans4mind.com/counterpoint/whiteley.shtml.

SARAH FLETCHER is an international mentoring consultant and director of the Institute of Mentoring and Coaching in Bath, U.K.

New Directions for Adult and Continuing Education • DOI: 10.1002/ace

What does the possible selves construct add to our understanding of adult learning and our capacity to foster it? Implications in relation to transformative learning are discussed.

8

Possible Selves in Adult Education

Marsha Rossiter

What can we conclude about how the possible selves construct may be useful to adult education practitioners and scholars? What does this perspective add to our understanding of learning in adulthood and our capacity to foster it? The contributors to this volume have offered a range of conceptual presentations of possible selves, any of which may suggest potential applications for adult educators. In this chapter, I summarize key considerations related to possible selves knowledge, comment on the possible selves perspective on transformative learning, and conclude with an overview of implications for adult educators.

Key Considerations Related to Possible Selves

As we review the previous chapters, one consideration that emerges pertains to factors that influence which possible selves are available to a person. While the hallmark of possible selves is, of course, possibility, it is clear that the possible is not unlimited. The contributions to this volume, particularly Chapter Five by Lips and Chapter Four by Lee and Oyserman, describe the socially constructed nature of selves considered to be possible. Cultural views of gender, race, sexual orientation, and socioeconomic status are indicators of societal marginalization. A sense of what is possible is defined by and bounded by a person's situated perspective—and if that perspective is situated at the margins of society, it is necessarily limited, shadowed by the dominant culture. Thus, socially constructed roles, the existence of contextual cues, levels of self-efficacy, and the availability of role models are

NEW DIRECTIONS FOR ADULT AND CONTINUING EDUCATION, no. 114, Summer 2007 © 2007 Wiley Periodicals, Inc.
Published online in Wiley InterScience (www.interscience.wiley.com) • DOI: 10.1002/ace.259

among the factors that shape and sometimes limit the repertoire of possible selves that an individual can envision.

A second consideration has to do with how, and under what circumstances, existing possible selves serve to motivate behavior. As indicated in several of the chapters, the level of elaborated detail associated with a possible self and the extent to which it is psychologically available to a person are factors that have an impact on whether the possible self has motivational power. We know from the work of Oyserman and her colleagues that a balance of a positive hoped-for self with a corresponding dreaded or feared possible self seems to be more strongly motivational than either the positive or negative possible self alone. Perceived alignment of a possible self with a sense of one's true self, as well as relevant efficacy beliefs, are also factors in how possible selves govern or organize behavior. Third, it is apparent from the previous chapters that multiple strategies are available to practitioners in working with the possible selves of students or clients in various practice settings. Specific interventions were described as means to assist persons to develop and detail positive possible selves.

Transformational and Transitional Learning

Probably the most fertile common ground shared by possible selves and adult education is in the realm of transformational and transitional learning. The very term possible selves implies the potential for change. The possible selves construct draws connections between the self-system and motivation to achieve goals between the current self and a sense of the self one might become. As such, it directly relates to and can deepen our understanding of the processes of transformational and transitional learning. While different views of transformational learning have been advanced (Mezirow, 1991, 2000; Freire, 1970; Tennant, 2000; Jarvis, 1992), the essential components of the process are (1) recognition of a need for change in one's life, perspectives, or circumstances; (2) critical reflection on individual or societal assumptions; (3) communication and connection with others who have a similar life experience; (4) exploration of what course of action is possible and desirable; and (5) enacting the new learning as an individual or through social action. Below is a discussion of transformational learning and related possible selves insights from the preceding chapters.

Letting Go. Several of the chapters in this volume, particularly Chapter Three by King and Hicks, call attention to the importance of the capacity to let go of old views of the self as one embraces a possible self. From their research, King and Hicks explain that persons who were able to more fully elaborate lost possible selves were better able to move on and embrace new possibilities. How does that relate to transformative learning? It seems plausible that the trigger for transformative learning—for example, the disorienting dilemma (Mezirow, 1991), the stimulating event (Cranton, 1994), or

the disjuncture between internal and external experience (Jarvis, 1992)—
may have a good deal to do with the "lost possible self" as discussed by King
and Hicks. Assuming that is the case, it would be useful in our ongoing dialogue regarding transformational learning theory to explore more fully the
process of letting go of existing meaning perspectives. Meaning perspectives,
defined by Mezirow (2000) as habits of thought or frames of reference, form
the foundation on which our sense of the possible and the desirable are
based. The scope and the boundaries of possibility, along with associated values, are defined by our meaning systems and habits of mind. We will not
construct expanded self-possibilities in a particular domain if we are operating within a mental framework that does not value, recognize, or even
encompass that domain. So an expanded meaning perspective is necessary
to envision and act on expanded possible selves.

But the move into the expanded framework carries some risk and
potential discomfort. Mezirow (1991) has described the result of transformative learning as movement toward meaning perspectives that are more
permeable and integrative. This is in accord with views of cognitive development understood as moving from the absolutism of duality toward multiplicity and relativism (Perry, 1981). The point is that integral to the
changes associated with transitional and transformative learning is the stepping forth out of a place of certainty and safety—where right is right and
wrong is wrong, and the boundary between is clear—into a territory of
tentative and partial truth at best. In the mental framework of absolutism,
one's sense of self also tends to be clear and stable: one is good or bad, right
or wrong, successful or a failure, and so on. While such a perspective carries with it constraints, it is also predictable and safe. So the transformation
process involves letting go of meaning perspectives that for many learners
have supported clear definitions of one's values and sense of self.

One implication for adult educators, then, is that in the possible selves
framework, we need to understand that a meaning perspective has a self-
concept dimension. A rejected or discarded meaning perspective is also a
rejected or discarded view of self. In transformational learning, adult learners are not just developing an expanded worldview and new ways of thinking about ideas. They are developing and realizing new possible selves.
Second, in working with adult learners, we need to encourage and enable
learners to fully articulate the meanings and the selves they are leaving
behind. In his well-known work on transitions, Bridges (1980) emphasizes
the point that transitions begin with endings. Disengagement, disidentifica-
tion, disenchantment, and disorientation are all part of the ending process in
his view. Bridges emphasizes the importance of taking time to process these
steps in the transitional experience. It is a disservice to students to expect
them to focus only on new, expanded perspectives and possible selves without due attention to the process of letting go of the selves they are no more.

Exploration. The possible selves construct also adds a dimension of
insight into the process of exploration of new possibilities by adult learners.

New Directions for Adult and Continuing Education • DOI: 10.1002/ace

One of the steps of transformative learning as outlined by Mezirow is the "exploration of options for new roles, relationships and actions" (2000, p. 22). As learners explore courses of action, they are formulating goals for themselves, operating with a future time perspective as Leondari described in Chapter Two. As we know, in adult education, we often see learners who are in the midst of a transition. The connection between life events and participation in adult education is well known. Divorce, loss of a job, change in health, and a new baby are among the many life events that require transition, learning, and adjustment. The possible selves perspective draws attention to the importance of the exploration stage of transformation or transition.

Again, it will be useful to turn to Bridges's conceptualization of transitions (1980), which he describes as beginning with an ending, moving through an in-between period, and ending with a new beginning. In this construal, the ending can be understood broadly as encompassing the trigger for transformative learning, and the new beginning can be related to the reintegration stages of transformative learning. The in-between period that Bridges identified corresponds with the transformative learning step of exploration of new options and experimenting with them. According to Bridges, during the in-between period, we are not altogether certain what the new circumstance will be like. It is a time of limbo and uncertainty. Bridges's advice is to take time to explore the other side of the transition and to accept uncertainty. He suggests that persons in transition "find out what is waiting in the wings of your life. Whether you chose your change or not, there are unlived potentialities within you, interests and talents that you have not yet explored. Transitions clear the ground for new growth" (p. 81).

Developing goals and a plan of action necessarily entails seeing oneself carrying out the action and achieving the goals. As several of the authors in this volume have discussed, people are more likely to take action in a particular domain if they have a well-developed possible self that is relevant to that domain. If an individual really cannot envision herself or himself doing something, it is unlikely that behavior will be directed toward that end. If it seems too far-fetched or too difficult, then it is merely a pipe dream, and it does not have motivational power to organize behavior.

Thus, transition to a new possible self is facilitated by visualizing and practicing the new self or the self having achieved a hoped-for goal. In Chapter Seven, Fletcher richly described a variety of practical approaches through which teachers and mentors can assist learners in practicing hoped-for possible selves. As athletes, performers, and public speakers have known for some time, picturing yourself actually doing, or having completed, what you hope to do creates a cognitive and emotional pathway to the achievement of the goal. The specific self-images serve as signposts along the way, and the attending feelings of joy and accomplishment stoke the motivational fire when energy runs low. Bridges advises persons in transition to project themselves into the expected future state: "Begin to identify yourself with the final result of the new beginning. What is it going to feel like when you've actually done whatever it is that you are setting out to do? All right, then, say it's done. There, you did it. You are the person who does that sort of thing. People look at you now as the one-who-did-it, and seeing yourself through their eyes, you realize what self-confidence is: experiencing yourself as one who can do things like that" (p. 146).

Another point to keep in mind in the consideration of possible selves and transition is that experimenting with possible selves may not be as rational and linear as we might assume. A criticism of Mezirow's transformation theory is that it tends to be too focused on the cognitive, rational, and sequential dimensions of the process (Dirkx, 1997; Taylor, 2000). In relation to career transition, Ibarra (2003) explains that in reality, it frequently involves a test-and-learn approach rather than the plan-and-implement model. That is, the actual experience of change for most people tends to be exploratory and inductive, in which possibilities and goals evolve throughout the process. This contrasts with prevalent prescriptions for life or career change that call for a more sequential, rational, deductive approach to progression toward an identified goal. In this way, Ibarra also calls attention to the middle territory of transition—the in-between period in which one is not what one used to be, but is not what one is going to be. In their discussion of career change in Chapter Six of this volume, Plimmer and Schmidt also highlight the role of possible selves in the process of transition. They point out that a well-developed possible self propels goal-directed action and serves as a guiding vision to help people weather the inevitable setbacks and adversity of a major transition. The point for adult educators here is that we need to take the time to assist adult learners in the process of envisioning and practicing possible selves. We need to understand that the exploration period is important, and it may not be linear and neat.

View of the Self. Implicit in the possible selves construct is the fact that learning stimulates and reflects changes in identity. Furthermore, it implies a view of the person as multidimensional and dynamic, rather than static and unitary, with ever unfolding potential throughout the life span. From this perspective, a number of selves have the potential to become actual at any particular time. In that sense, the possible selves orientation stands in contrast to the true-self model of identity. This is important to our practice as adult educators. As Clark and Dirkx (2000) have pointed out, the idea of self—how we conceptualize the self—is "foundational to how we think about and theorize learning" (p. 101).

The field of adult education has been historically grounded in a humanistic view of the person's potential for self-development as an integrated autonomous agent. The assumptions of Knowles's andragogy (1980) regarding the self-directed and internally motivated adult learner reflect that stance. But more recently leaders in the field have questioned that view of the self and the associated purposes of adult education. Tennant (2000), for example, advances the position that "the conventional view of adult education as cultivating a self that is independent, rational, autonomous, and coherent is no longer sustainable in a world characterized by difference and diversity" (p. 99). His point is that such a view does not accommodate a diversity of perspectives and views of adulthood and therefore is less than inclusive. He suggests that a narrative view of self and life span development is one alternative to the individualistic orientation that is more congruent with the prevalent practices in adult education.

More recently, narrative meaning making and narrative learning have been explored in relation to adult education practice (Rossiter and Clark, 2007). Clearly the possible selves perspective is congruent with a narrative understanding of identity in which the self is understood as an unfolding story rather than as a static state. We can understand the development and elaboration of possible selves as a process of self-storying. In a related vein, Randall (1996) has described transformative learning as the process of restorying one's self or one's life. A key component of the narrative understanding of identity development is the concept of self-authoring—the idea that individuals can exercise some choice in guiding their own development and shaping their own life narrative. Mezirow (2000) describes transformative learning as a shift toward a self-authoring frame of reference. And Kegan (2000) goes on to frame such learning as a shift in epistemological orientation from being acted on or being "made up by" external forces in the socializing orientation to acting on or "writing on" in the self-authoring orientation (p. 59). The main point is that the narrative orientation is empowering in its attention to self-authorship. To the extent that we understand the identification, elaboration, and motivation to realize possible selves as part of the self-storying process, we can appreciate the role of possible selves in the construction of the life narrative.

Conclusion

Overall, what does the possible selves perspective mean for adult teaching and learning? First, because our position as educators—teachers, mentors, learning guides—is one of relative power, we ought not underestimate the impact of our feedback on some adult learners. Students tend to attribute significance to the comments, behaviors, and attitudes of certain teachers, mentors, and advisers (Rossiter, 2004; Brookfield, 1990). It is therefore important for adult educators to speak honestly to adult learners about their potential and possible selves. Perhaps we typically do not give adequate consideration to this dynamic. When we as educators articulate a potential goal or possibility for a learner, this can serve to elevate the status of the possibility in the learner's cognition from a pipe dream into the realm of the achievable. This movement from dream to achievable status as a possible self activates motivation. As the chapter authors have written, the more well-elaborated and psychologically accessible a possible self is, the more motivationally powerful it is. What adult educators can do is to assist learners in the development of a very faint sense of potential into a detailed, challenging, and achievable possibility.

Second, the possible selves perspective offers an alternative perspective on the adult learning process that mediates transition and transformation. This view highlights an adult learner's future-oriented self-concept as a motivating and organizing factor in transformational learning. The emergence of new possible selves marks and defines the incremental expansion of the learner's sense of possibility. Possible selves provide the stepping stones, the scaffolding, by which an adult student is able to grow, change, cast off constraints, and take on new challenges (Rossiter, 2004).

Third, educators and other helpers can be particularly influential in planting the seeds for new possibilities. The process of transformational learning involves some capacity to reflect on one's current state, explore new ways of being or thinking, and incorporate those new perspectives into one's life action. The process is not complete without this praxis, which requires not only a transformed perspective on the world but also a transformed sense of self-in-the-world. Envisioning different courses of action and roles, each of which involves a particular possible self, is the action of the exploration stage of transformational learning. Relationships with teachers, mentors, and advisers are especially important, as they may be the focus of observational learning by students. Individuals look to role models for attitudes, perspectives and behaviors through which to develop a new possibility.

Fourth, transition involves rehearsing attitudes and behaviors, visualizing oneself as having achieved a hoped-for goal represented by a possible self. Rehearsing and visualizing enable one to assess one's own comfort with moving in that direction. It is at this point that some possibilities are discarded and others more fully embraced. As a possible self is more highly elaborated, it becomes more operative in one's working self-concept. In other words, motivated action toward the goal increases as the possible self is more detailed and accessible in one's consciousness. Understanding this dynamic, we as educators can be more purposeful, intentional, and skillful in helping learners develop and practice a possible self.

The chapter authors have outlined the usefulness of the idea of possible selves in understanding adult learner motivation and persistence. We can appreciate possible selves as expressions of adult learners' educational, career, and personal goals. And we can conclude that teachers, mentors, and advisers in adult education play an important part in enabling adult learners to envision and elaborate possibilities for their future. The construction of possible selves is a central dynamic in transformational and transitional learning. In sum, it seems clear that the possible selves construct can contribute to our understanding of adult learning.

References

Bridges, W. *Transitions: Making Sense of Life's Changes.* Reading, Mass.: Addison-Wesley, 1980.

Brookfield, S. *The Skillful Teacher.* San Francisco: Jossey-Bass, 1990.

Clark, M. C., and Dirkx, J. M. "Moving Beyond a Unitary Self: A Reflective Dialogue." In A. L. Wilson and E. R. Hayes (eds.), *Handbook of Adult and Continuing Education.* San Francisco: Jossey-Bass, 2000.

Cranton, P. *Understanding and Promoting Transformative Learning: A Guide for Educators of Adults.* San Francisco: Jossey-Bass, 1994.

Dirkx, J. M. "Nurturing Soul in Adult Learning." In P. Cranton (ed.), *Transformative Learning in Action: Insights from Practice.* New Directions for Adult and Continuing Education, no. 74. San Francisco: Jossey-Bass, 1997.

Freire, P. *Pedagogy of the Oppressed.* New York: Seabury Press, 1970.

Ibarra, H. *Working Identity: Unconventional Strategies for Reinventing Your Career.* Boston: Harvard Business School Press, 2003.

Jarvis, P. *Paradoxes of Learning: On Becoming an Individual in Society.* San Francisco: Jossey-Bass, 1992.

Kegan, R. "What 'Form' Transforms? A Constructive-Developmental Approach to Transformative Learning." In J. Mezirow and Associates, *Learning as Transformation: Critical Perspectives on a Theory in Progress.* San Francisco: Jossey-Bass, 2000.

Knowles, M.S. *The Modern Practice of Adult Education: From Pedagogy to Andragogy.* (Rev. and updated.) Cambridge: Adult Education Company, 1980.

Mezirow, J. *Transformative Dimensions of Adult Learning.* San Francisco: Jossey-Bass, 1991.

Mezirow, J. "Learning to Think Like an Adult." In J. Mezirow and Associates, *Learning as Transformation: Critical Perspectives on a Theory in Progress.* San Francisco: Jossey-Bass, 2000.

Perry, W. G. "Cognitive and Ethical Growth: The Making of Meaning." In A. W. Chickering (ed.), *The Modern American College.* San Francisco: Jossey-Bass, 1981.

Randall, W. "Restorying a Life: Adult Education and Transformative Learning." In J. E. Birren and others (eds.), *Aging and Biography: Explorations in Adult Development.* New York: Springer, 1996.

Rossiter, M. "Educational Relationships and Possible Selves in the Adult Undergraduate Experience." In R. M. Cervero, B. C. Courtenay, M. T. Hixson, and J. S. Valente (eds.), *The Cyril O. Houle Scholars in Adult and Continuing Education Program Global Research Perspectives: Volume 4.* Athens, GA: The University of Georgia, 2004.

Rossiter, M., and Clark, M. C. *Narrative and the Practice of Adult Education.* Malabar, Fla.: Krieger, 2007.

Taylor, E. W. "Analyzing Research on Transformative Learning Theory." In J. Mezirow and Associates, *Learning as Transformation: Critical Perspectives on a Theory in Progress.* San Francisco: Jossey-Bass, 2000.

Tennant, M. "Adult Learning for Self-Development and Change." In A. L. Wilson and E. R. Hayes (eds.), *Handbook of Adult and Continuing Education.* San Francisco: Jossey-Bass, 2000.

MARSHA ROSSITER *is assistant vice chancellor for lifelong learning and community engagement at the University of Wisconsin Oshkosh.*

INDEX

research and from that of practitioners who see themselves as working toward authentic practice.

The contributors address five overlapping and interrelated dimensions of authenticity: self-awareness and self-exploration; awareness of others (especially students); relationships with students; awareness of cultural, social, and educational contexts and their influence on practice; and critical self-reflection on teaching.

ISBN 0-7879-9403-0

ACE110 The Neuroscience of Adult Learning
Sandra Johnson and Kathleen Taylor

Recent research developments have added much to our understanding of brain function. Though some neurobiologists have explored implications for learning, few have focused on learning in adulthood. This issue of New Directions for Adult and Continuing Education, *The Neuroscience of Adult Learning,* examines links between this emerging research and adult educators' practice. Now that it is possible to trace the pathways of the brain involved in various learning tasks, we can also explore which learning environments are likely to be most effective. Volume contributors include neurobiologists, educators, and clinical psychologists who have illuminated connections between how the brain functions and how to enhance learning. Among the topics explored here are basic brain architecture and "executive" functions of the brain, how learning can "repair" the effects of psychological trauma on the brain, effects of stress and emotions on learning, the centrality of experience to learning and construction of knowledge, the mentor-learner relationship, and intersections between best practices in adult learning and current neurobiological discoveries. Although the immediate goal of this volume is to expand the discourse on teaching and learning practices, our overarching goal is to encourage adult learners toward more complex ways of knowing.

ISBN 0-7879-8704-2

ACE109 Teaching for Change: Fostering Transformative Learning in the Classroom
Edward W. Taylor

Fostering transformative learning is about teaching for change. It is not an approach to be taken lightly, arbitrarily, or without much thought. Many would argue that it requires intentional action, a willingness to take personal risk, a genuine concern for the learners' betterment, and the wherewithal to draw on a variety of methods and techniques that help create a classroom environment that encourages and supports personal growth. What makes the work of transformative learning even more difficult is the lack of clear signposts or guidelines that teachers can follow when they try to teach for change. There is now a need to return to the classroom and look through the lens of those who have been engaged in the practice of fostering transformative learning. This volume's authors are seasoned practitioners and scholars who have grappled with the fundamental issues associated with teaching for change (emotion, expressive ways of knowing, power, cultural difference, context, teacher authenticity, spirituality) in a formal classroom setting; introduced innovations that enhance the practice of fostering transformative learning; and asked ethical questions that need to be explored and reflected upon when practicing transformative learning in the classroom.

ISBN 0-7879-8584-8

ACE108 **Adulthood: New Terrain**
Mary Alice Wolf
One of the many surprises about the lifespan perspective is that individuals, families, institutions, and corporations lead *many* lives. The purpose of this resource is to acquaint and update practitioners in adult education and related roles with emerging and creative methods of 1) appreciating the learner's perspective, 2) moderating content and learning format to enhance meaning-making in the learning environment, and 3) developing tools to address alternative modes of development and growth that occur in adulthood and challenge adult educators on a daily basis.

What does the new adult learner look like? This volume contains theory and research on learners who turn to educational programs in times of transition and explores ways of connecting with new cognitive and affective meanings.

This volume explores dimensions of adult development from ethnographic, research, and theoretical perspectives. It addresses adult learners' experience and meaning of education as an ongoing resource for well-being and positive development across the lifecourse. It updates the reader in the emerging terrain of adulthood; adult learning philosophies are implemented and modified to meet adults' developmental mandate to continue learning in order to make meaning and find purpose during the countless transitions of the ever-increasing adult years.
ISBN 0-7879-8396-0

ACE107 **Artistic Ways of Knowing: Expanded Opportunities for Teaching and Learning**
Randee Lipson Lawrence
This volume of *New Directions for Adult and Continuing Education* challenges the dominant paradigm of how knowledge is typically constructed and shared in adult education settings by focusing on ways in which adult educators can expand learning opportunities and experiences for their learners. Art appeals universally to us all and has the capacity to bridge cultural differences. Art can also foster individual and social transformation, promoting dialogue and deepening awareness of ourselves and the world around us. The contributors to this volume include actors, musicians, photographers, storytellers, and poets, all of whom also happen to be adult educators. In each chapter, the author describes how one or more forms of artistic expression were used to promote learning in formal or informal adult education settings. In each case, the purpose of education was not to teach art (that is, not to develop expertise in acting, poetry writing, or creating great works of art). Conversely, art was used as a means to access learning in subjects as divergent as English language acquisition, action research, community awareness, and social justice.
ISBN 0-7879-8284-9

ACE106 **Class Concerns: Adult Education and Social Class**
Tom Nesbitt
This volume of *New Directions for Adult and Continuing Education* brings together several leading progressive adult educators to explore how class affects different arenas of adult education practice and discourse. It highlights the links between adult education, the material and social conditions of daily and working lives, and the economic and political systems that underpin them. Chapters focus on adult education policies;

teaching; learning and identity formation; educational institutions and social movements; and the relationships between class, gender, and race. Overall, the volume reaffirms the salience of class in shaping the lives we lead and the educational approaches we develop. It offers suggestions for adult educators to identify and resist the encroachments of global capitalism and understand the role of education in promoting social equality. Finally, it suggests that a class perspective can provide an antidote to much of the social amnesia, self-absorption, and apolitical theorizing that pervades current adult education discourse.
ISBN 0-7879-8128-1

ACE105 HIV/AIDS Education for Adults
John P. Egan

Contributors from the United States, Canada, and Australia, working in university-based and community-based environments and for divergent communities—present specific experiences in the fight against HIV/AIDS. They share stories of shifting paradigms and challenging norms, and of seeking and finding innovation. Topics examined include the struggle for meaning and power in HIV/AIDS education, HIV prevention workers and injection drug users, community-based research, grassroots response to HIV/AIDS in Nova Scotia, sex workers and HIV/AIDS education, and the Tuskegee Syphilis Study and legacy recruitment for experimental vaccines. By examining HIV/AIDS through an adult education lens, we gain insights into how communities (and governments) can respond quickly and effectively to emergent health issues—and other issues linked to marginalization.
ISBN 0-7879-8032-3

ACE104 Embracing and Enhancing the Margins of Adult Education
Meg Wise, Michelle Glowacki-Dudka

Adult educators increasingly risk and resist being placed at the margins of academic and other organizations. This volume argues that depending on how those margins are defined, margins can be a place of creativity and power from which to examine and challenge dominant ideology and practice. Chapters explore advances and effective practices being made in the margins of adult education from several perspectives including community-based programs, interreligious learning, human resource development, African American underrepresentation in the academy, and degree-granting adult education programs. Other areas explored include an interdisciplinary Web-based patient education research program and educational focus on citizenship and public responsibility skills.
ISBN 0-7879-7859-0

ACE103 Developing and Delivering Adult Degree Programs
James P. Pappas, Jerry Jerman

The explosive growth in adult degree programs is fueled by increased distance education technologies, potential for providing additional revenue streams for institutions, fierce competition from the private sector and from other higher education institutions, and rising interest in interdisciplinary programs. This issue explores adult degree programs and considers the theoretical underpinnings of such programs and hands-on issues as curriculum, faculty, marketing, technology, financing, and accreditation, all with a goal of informing and equipping both scholars and practitioners.
ISBN 0-7879-7767-5

NEW DIRECTIONS FOR ADULT & CONTINUING EDUCATION
Order Form
SUBSCRIPTIONS AND SINGLE ISSUES

DISCOUNTED BACK ISSUES:

Use this form to receive **20% off** *all back issues of New Directions for Adult & Continuing Education. All single issues priced at* **$23.20** *(normally $29.00)*

TITLE   ISSUE NO.   ISBN

_____   _____   _____

_____   _____   _____

_____   _____   _____

Call **888-378-2537** *or see mailing instructions below. When calling, mention the promotional code, JB7ND, to receive your discount.*

SUBSCRIPTIONS: *(1 year, 4 issues)*

☐ New Order   ☐ Renewal

U.S.	☐ Individual: $80	☐ Institutional: $195
Canada/Mexico	☐ Individual: $80	☐ Institutional: $235
All Others	☐ Individual: $104	☐ Institutional: $269

Call **888-378-2537** *or see mailing and pricing instructions below. Online subscriptions are available at www.interscience.wiley.com.*

Copy or detach page and send to:
**John Wiley & Sons, Journals Dept, 5th Floor
989 Market Street, San Francisco, CA 94103-1741**

Order Form can also be faxed to: 888-481-2665

Issue/Subscription Amount: $ _____	**SHIPPING CHARGES:**
Shipping Amount: $ _____	SURFACE Domestic Canadian
(for single issues only—subscription prices include shipping)	First Item $5.00 $6.00
Total Amount: $ _____	Each Add'l Item $3.00 $1.50

(No sales tax for U.S. subscriptions. Canadian residents, add GST for subscription orders. Individual rate subscriptions must be paid by personal check or credit card. Individual rate subscriptions may not be resold as library copies.)

☐ Payment enclosed (U.S. check or money order only. All payments must be in U.S. dollars.)

☐ VISA   ☐ MC   ☐ Amex # _____ Exp. Date _____

Card Holder Name _____ Card Issue # _____

Signature_____ Day Phone _____

☐ Bill Me (U.S. institutional orders only. Purchase order required.)

Purchase order # _____
              Federal Tax ID13559302   GST 89102 8052

Name_____

Address _____

Phone _____ E-mail _____